The Novels of Manohar Malgonkar

By the same author

The Novels of Bernard Malamud (1988)

The Novels of Manohar Malgonkar

A Study in the Quest for Fulfilment

M. Rajagopalachari

PRESTIGE

Published by
Prestige Books
3/28, East Patel Nagar, New Delhi 110 008
in association with
Indian Society for Commonwealth Studies
New Delhi

ISBN 81-85218-16-1
Price:

Jacket design by
3-A Corporation,
New Delhi 110 002

Phototypesetting by
data culture
New Delhi 110 065
Ph. 6431070

Printed by
Efficient Offset Printers
Delhi

Contents

Preface

Despite Malgonkar's breadth of vision and commendable technique evidenced in the fictional and the empirical modes of creation, he has received far less critical evaluation than his due. Today there are only two full-length critical studies by Amur and Dayananda. Brief references could be found in the works of Srinivasa Iyengar, Raji Narsimhan, V.S. Naipaul and Meenakshi Mukherjee besides a few articles in the Periodicals. Critics in general have acclaimed the appealing directness and sincerity of Malgonkar's narrative pattern and the authentic evocation of the turbulent years of freedom struggle in his novels although they have reservations about his overambitious preoccupation with dramatic effect. Also there have been a few sweeping generalisations on the basis of a single aspect. Paul Verghese, for example, says that Malgonkar's weakness is that he concentrates more "on the exotic and melodramatic than on the worthwhile aspects of modern life." Meenakshi Mukherjee dismisses *A Bend in the Ganges* as no better than "a skilful reportage." Raji Narsimhan finds fault with his white characters "as no more than brown *sahebs* in the reverse with blemishes and complexities ironed out." There has been thus a mixture of adulation and bitterness in their remarks. Amur is not wide off the mark when he comments that the criticism of Malgonkar's work is a "good illustration of the prejudices and preconceptions" which have often come in the way of a just assessment of Indian writing in English.

However Amur and Dayananda have attempted a balanced appraisal of Malgonkar's novels. They have made a general critical evaluation of the several themes and aspects of his fictional technique. Yet an effort could be made to study Malgonkar's characterisation which at the base reveals an agonising quest for fulfilment. In order to get a balanced view of the author's achievement, his major fiction is studied here to bring out the theme of fulfilment that has shaped his characters and hence his novels.

Almost all the major characters of Malgonkar have in them "an irresistible urge for fulfilment." Whether the fulfilment is sought in love or in revenge, in compassion or in commitment, the urge becomes predominant and renders every other aspect subsidiary. The characters evince a certain measure of courage and maturity, and struggle against the odds of life to gain a sense of fulfilment. This agonising quest imparts the characters vigour and force.

Chapter I broadly outlines Malgonkar's idea of fiction, and sums up the critical scholarship. Story-telling is the organic principle of Malgonkar's fictional technique. The story, action and plot centre round a major character marked with an intense quest for fulfilment. The chapter also points out how the various characters in his different novels seek fulfilment. Malgonkar's affinity with Henry James and John Masters is commented upon.

Chapter II is an analysis of *Distant Drum* which reveals a soldier's fulfilment in commitment to duty. In his steadfast commitment and integrity, Kiran the hero of the novel surpasses with distinction his British ideal Ropey Booker. Unlike Ropey, he finds fulfilment in his duty in spite of heavy odds.

Chapter III brings out how Henry Winton in *Combat of Shadows* fails miserably because of the conflict between "desire and aversion." A man of no integrity, Winton fails to realise his fulfilment in love. On the contrary Ruby Miranda, an Anglo-Indian girl, emerges successfully with a sense of fulfilment in revenge. She is avenged on Henry for the humiliation he had inflicted upon her by his sudden rejection of her love.

Chapter IV analyses *The Princes* to bring out the fulfilment of Prince Abhayraj in the old order in spite of his awareness of its fast disintegration by the Instrument of Accession Act. Abhayraj, though apparently modern, identifies himself with the values which his father cherished. This completes the process of identification.

Chapter V on *A Bend in the Ganges* shows the overpowering nature of love which imparts fulfilment to the two major characters, Gian and Debidayal. Malgonkar dismisses violence as a way of life revealing its self-consuming nature through Debidayal. By making Gian an ironic symbol of non-violence, he subtly comments on its importance through the technique of indirection or "deflection." However, he seems to conclude that no single compact ideology can be a panacea to the many inexplicable problems of life.

Chapter VI on *The Devil's Wind* reveals Malgonkar's treatment of historical facts. Malgonkar defends Nana Saheb and exonerates him from the various crimes foisted on him. Nana, according to him, is not the arch-villain of the Sepoy Revolt as distorted by the British, but a humane personality who sought fulfilment in compassion, love and patriotism. He has compassion even for the British especially women and children. But by a historic accident, Nana is associated with the gruesome murders of which he was not guilty.

A detailed note on *The Garland Keepers,* Malgonkar's latest novel, is appended at the end.

A study of Malgonkar's novels brings out his humane vision of life and broad canvas of his work. He appears to emphasise that integrity alone gives fulfilment. Though he insists on "felt experience," he maintains discrete aesthetic distance in the delineation of characters. The study has made use of Malgonkar's views on his art while interpreting his fictional mode in the light of the dominant theme of fulfilment. In my view, all his important novels demonstrate the complexity of human existence as the characters enter the vortex of experience driven by the urge for fulfilment.

I cannot close these prefatory remarks without expressing my gratitude to all those who have helped me in the preparation of the present books. I am grateful to my teacher Dr. S. Laxmana Murthy, Professor of English, Kakatiya University for his affectionate advice and help. He has been for me over the years an unfailing source of inspiration. I am thankful to Professor Satyanarain Singh for his keen interest in the progress of my work.

My thanks are due to Professor James Y. Dayananda (Lock-haven State College, Pennsylvania) who has kindly sent me the reprints of his important articles on Magonkar. I am highly obliged to Dr. R.K. Dhawan of Delhi University for his friendly help and advice, especially about the format of the book.

I thank M/s Prestige Books, New Delhi for printing this book neatly and promptly.

A Teller of Tales

Manohar Malgonkar is a prominent Indo-English novelist. He has made a distinct contribution to Indian writing in English as "a down-to-earth teller of tales."[1] He has published ten novels, three collections of short stories, three histories, three works of non-fiction and a play. Of the ten novels, six merit serious literary consideration. The first four novels were published within five years, viz. *Distant Drum* (1960), *Combat of Shadows* (1962), *The Princes* (1963), *A Bend in the Ganges* (1964), which as Srinivasa Iyengar points out, show "a certain maturity about them, and in plotting as well as in telling his stories he displays an ability that compels recognition."[2] *The Devil's Wind* (1972) is the story of Nana Saheb, the controversial figure of the Sepoy Revolt of 1857. *The Garland Keepers* (1986), his latest, is a novel on Emergency. Malgonkar wrote *A Spy in Amber* as a screen-play for a Hindi film which his daughter subsequently drafted into a novel. *Shalimar* is Malgonkar's novelisation of Krishna Shah's film story. *Open Season* written originally as film story was later made into a novel. *Bandicoot Run* is a detective story.

Malgonkar has earned a niche for himself in Indo-English fiction by his compelling "story telling" technique and the probing insight into life. Though his output is limited, his achievement in the fictional and the empirical modes of creation is not any the less compared to any other Indian novelist writing in English. He is one of those few writers who gain the stamp of unmistakable authenticity by transmuting "felt experience"[3] into art. His own diverse experiences in the fields of big-game hunting, civil service, army, business and politics have helped him catch the "color of life"[4] especially of the upper strata.

Malgonkar reduces the organic principle of his fictional technique to "story-telling." He seems to believe like Conrad that the novel could be an expansion of a "yarn" or a short-story.[5] Malgonkar defines his effort:

I do strive deliberately and hard, to tell a story well; and I revel in incident, in improbabilities, in unexpected twists. I feel a special allegiance to this particular sub-caste among those whose caste-mark I have affected, the entertainers, the tellers of stories.[6]

Novels which do not conform to this basic pattern do not constitute a "square meal" for Malgonkar.[7] In his emphasis on story-telling, he comes close to endorsing Henry James's dictum that "the story and the novel, the idea and the form, are the needle and thread."[8] His antipathy, therefore, to the psychological novel of Virginia Woolf and James Joyce is quite understandable. Malgonkar identifies the novel with story, plot, action and not with the ramblings of the mind.

I often think myself as belonging to the advance guard in the swing-back of the romantic novel. The pedlars of erosion and drug dreams may churn out bestsellers, but these are not novels, and the interminable ramblings about the day in the life of some one or other are like counting the veins in every leaf of cabbage. All this was a phase, but you cannot play with a cabbage for long. The novel will be back, story, plot, and all the signs are already there.[9]

The plotless kind ot novel with all its intricacies of technique holds no attraction for Malgonkar. The problem of expression has engaged Malgonkar's attention and he has an acute insight into what a novelist can do in a language he is not born to. One can, of course, exploit very masterfully the nuances of one's own language, but denied this advantage in an alien tongue, one has the need to look for other avenues like story, plot and action to sustain the fabric. Malgonkar thus discerns an additional and compelling need in defence of story, and depends on his own skill "to push forward the plot, on my craftsmanship as a novelist."[10] He admires writers like John P. Marquand, Truman Capote, Steinbeck, Graham Green, Hemingway, Faulkner, E.M. Forster, R.K. Narayan as "excellent story-tellers" and that their novels are "well-constructed, are dramatic, and they are not afraid of incident."[11] Malgonkar's novels are packed with action and drama, and it is in the interaction of the characters with a series of events and incidents that they hold the reader's interest. His plots conform to Walter O'Grady's view that a plot is not so much a structure which suggests something static as it is a process—the continuing, inter-relatedness of the exterior situations, incidents, and the interior states of mind, events.[12] In this process, the characters undergo change and vibrate with life.

If a novelist's maturity is said to be displayed in his talent to offer, by way of events, "a community of individual lives in the act of defining themselves,"[13] Malgonkar can be called a mature novelist. His fictional pattern manifests vital situations for the characters to discover their identity through the "irresistible urge for fulfilment."[14] The action of the novels in its various events and incidents becomes significant in so far as it helps the characters grow to assert their identity. Malgonkar's characters and incidents are so interdependent in fiction that his technique exemplifies Henry James's comment that character is the determination of incident and incident the illustration of character.[15]

D.R. Sharma finds in the novels of Malgonkar dramatization of "the Satpura code" underscoring the moral values of "daring and decency." He is of the opinion that all the protagonists except Henry Winton of *Combat of Shadows* subscribe to this code. Sharma argues that in the case of *Combat of Shadows*, Malgonkar suggests the value of code through its negation.[16] It is somewhat laboured to stretch the Satpura code of the army of all the novels by making it all-comprehensive. Malgonkar's characters in fact do not subscribe themselves to any rigid code. On the contrary, they strive to seek fulfilment in whatever they believe. The quest for fulfilment in the main defines the life-pattern of Malgonkar's characters. The army officer Kiran in *Distant Drum* seeks his fulfilment in "living up to the code of honour" maintained by his Regimental life. He faces the challenges of life without yielding himself to undue pressures and ultimately wins Bina, his girl-friend. Henry Winton in *Combat of Shadows* tries to seek fulfilment in his love for an Anglo-Indian girl Ruby Miranda, but fails miserably because of his own conflict between "desire and aversion," and his moral depravity. Ruby Miranda, Kistulal and Sudden Dart, all affected in many ways by Henry's evil machinations, seek fulfilment in fierce revenge. Prince Abhayraj in *The Princes* struggles in vain to find his fulfilment in keeping up the old order which was ready to fall like "ripe mangoes in late May." The two major characters Gian and Debidayal in *A Bend in the Ganges* could find their fulfilment neither in violence nor in non-violence but in the over-powering bliss of love. The historic character

Nana Saheb in *The Devil's Wind* finds fulfilment in the human values of friendship, compassion and love. Thus all the major characters of Malgonkar's novels pulsate with life because of their irresistible urge for fulfilment. The aim of the present study is to evaluate the theme of fulfilment as realised through character, event and incident.

Malgokar is very often described as "the John Masters of the Indo-English Fiction,"[17] chiefly because of his affinity in matters of historic authenticity and gripping drama. But the much-discussed comparison between John Masters and Malgonkar need not be confined to the terms of the historic authenticity alone. It is valid also because of their characters's passionate struggle to discover their identity. John Cotton's comment on John Masters's characters could very well apply to those of Malgonkar. Cotton writes:

> They suffer doubts and heart-searchings as well as fears and privations; their quest is as much for identity or relationships as for the enemy or the spy.[18]

John Masters's *Bhowani Junction*, for example, portrays quite dexterously the predicament of an Anglo-Indian's searching for roots in the rapidly crumbling British India. The Anglo-Indian girl Victoria Jones could become neither English nor Indian completely though she finally opts for a Britisher. Malgonkar's *Combat of Shadows* presents a sensitive understanding of the relationship between the Anglo-Indians and the British officers in the rapidly changing India. It depicts the unrealised hopes of an Anglo-Indian girl Ruby Miranda, to establish herself as a *memsahib* in the world of the British.

Masters's *Nightrunners of Bengal* and Malgonkar's *The Devil's Wind* deal with the historic Sepoy Revolt of 1857. Malgonkar does not agree with the view that Masters's *Nightrunners of Bengal* is "the best historical novel about the Indian Mutiny."[19] He is not happy with the historical accuracy of John Masters's novel. He comments:

> He (John Masters) writes about the rebellion as though it were a mutiny, he writes about us Indians as the enemy, and he wanted, naturally, the British ruler of the Companies to be perpetuated, whereas my viewpoint is so opposite in this novel *(The Devil's Wind)* at all times, that there was no possibility of any agreement,

on our viewpoints at least.[20]

Despite their divergent points of view in regard to the role of history, both Malgonkar and Masters render the theme of self-discovery with great narrative skill in their fiction.

Malgonkar has affinity with John Marquand. Malgonkar himself has admitted Marquand's impact on the craft, form and style of his fiction. He also seems to write like Marquand "as a learned man about other learned men."[21] We, therefore, find in Malgonkar the inside picture of the princes, soldiers and British officers, and not of the coolies and untouchables as in Mulk Raj Anand. The few characters of the lower strata like Kanakchand, Gauri, Kistulal, Aji, Mumtaz do not give us the feel of a realised life. It is, perhaps, the reason why his writings are considered "withdrawn" from the reality of his country's poverty. Malgonkar acknowledges the fact:

> The social life of millions of Indians centres round the dustbins of great cities. Granted. But mine doesn't, and for me to write about it would be as insincere as a white man writing about a Negro riot.[22]

His own army service and princely ancestry brought him into close contact with "the living English" and the upper class of people. Malgonkar's insistence on the authenticity of felt experience keeps him within the confines of direct involvement.

Like a dramatist, Malgonkar deliberately keeps in mind the nature and taste of his audience or readers.[23] Though he says that he writes to be accepted by the English and American readers, he invariably draws upon the reserves of the Indian ethos and milieu to win authenticity and accuracy.

> I keep writing of India . . . because I feel no author should write outside his own living circumstances. If he does, it is phoney.[24]

His descriptions of the princely life and its pomp and glory, and finally its disintegration in *The Princes,* of the army life and war scenes in *Distant Drum,* of the dark interiors of the Indian jungles and wild-life hunting in *Combat of Shadows,* of the Partition of India and the consequent Hindu-Muslim riots in *A Bend in the Ganges,* of Nana's involvement in the process of history in *The Devil's Wind*—all reveal a deep concern for authenticity informed by a verve of personal knowledge.

Malgonkar's ideas on the role of history in fiction agree with those of Henry James. He appears to share with James that "as the picture is reality, so the novel is history."[25] Henry James refutes the belief that the novelist is less occupied in looking for the truth than the historian. He believes that

> The subject matter of fiction is stored up likewise in documents and records, and if it will not give itself away, as they say in California, it must speak with assurance, with the tone of the historian.[26]

Malgonkar too feels that history and fiction have many elements in common, and asserts that history forms the basis of most of his work.[27] He says that his novels are "close enough to the ground to pass off for straight history."[28] He writes:

> I take great pains to be absolutely accurate. If I write that something happened on a Saturday or on a moonless night, you can be sure it was on a Saturday or on a moonless night.[29]

Both James and Malgonkar believe in the authentic historic value that a creative work carries with it. Malgonkar's attempt in his historical novels like *The Princes* and *The Devil's Wind* is evidently to "make even history certainly readable."[30] His historical works—*Kanhoji Angrey* (1959) reissued as *The Sea-Hawk*, *Puars of Dewas Senior* (1969), and *Chhatrapatis of Kolhapur* (1971), though not very original, reveal Malgonkar's keen and intelligent sense of history.

Besides the authentic historicity Malgonkar has deep awareness of the technique of characterisation in shaping the story. Commenting on the process of characterisation, Malgonkar says:

> I thought they were sufficiently camouflaged for you not to think of them as real persons. They are actually composite personalities, you know; there is no real person. I might disguise the voice or size of the person and put them into a character which has absolutely

no connection with that person. And I think that the mental process is not deliberate at all . . . it's rather involved and you just arrive at it. What I can speak more authoritatively on is 'How to make a fictional person into a real person.' Take a character like Minnie for instance. And give her the sort of composite attributes of people whom you have met in real life. So that to the reader she appears as some real person you have described.[31]

It is by this technique of camouflage that Malgonkar successfully creates what Henry James has called "the illusion of life."[32] The Maharaja of Begwad, Abhayraj, Henry Winton, Kiran, Debidayal, Gian—all are composite portraits who take their cue from Malgonkar's personal knowledge of various princes, soldiers, British officers and Anglo-Indians. However, in the case of Nana Saheb, Malgonkar turns a real character into a fictional one with his imaginative insight.

Malgonkar analyses the characters and events with a bit of detachment characteristic of a historian. This has provoked Shakti Batra to indict Malgonkar's characters as "faceless" and "conventional."[33] Batra complains:

> Malgonkar's account takes the form of a cool, impersonal debate among the characters; it looks like a scientific analysis of the situation rather than something which emerges out of the characters themselves and their conviction.[34]

While dramatising his own experiences and knowledge of history, the writer is rather bound to maintain discrete aesthetic distance with the characters and events depicted in his works. In his first novel *Distant Drum* he fails to keep this distance in certain parts by resorting to elaborate descriptions of war scenes. But even there as in other novels, we find the characters emerging in flesh and blood, affirming their identity in their interaction with events.

Dayananda believes that Malgonkar's problem lies in the adaptation of a story-telling skill to historical subjects.[35] In his novels Malgonkar seeks artistic integration of his experience and history within the framework of fiction. *The Princes* is the culmination of this artistic integrity and hence his masterpiece. Except in *Distant Drum* which in parts tends to be a mere reportage of army life, Malgonkar successfully presents a harmonious blend of history and fiction in all his novels. It is difficult to agree with Dayananda's view that *A Bend in the Ganges* droops because story and history do not blend.[36] The novel at once depicts the horror of the Partition days and evaluates the ideologies of violence and non-violence in the given historic context and human life as a whole. It also shows through sensitive characters like Gian and Debidayal, how the ideologies shut off from the reality of life cannot face the challenges of life. Thematically the novel reflects the author's keener perception of life. It may seem to want the symmetry of *The Princes*. Nevertheless the characterisation and the story are in tune with the historical background. *Combat of Shadows* explores the relationship between the Indians and the British through the conflict caused in the protagonist Henry Winton by his fear to cross the "thin line" that separates managers from their employees. The division of the novel into two major parts marking the turn of events in Henry Winton's life, gives the novel "the neat symmetry of the hourglass."[37] *The Devil's Wind* shows the artistic exploitation of historical fact through the poignant story of Nana Saheb.

It is also quite interesting to note how Malgonkar uses the point of view technique in his novels. With the exception of *The Princes* and *The Devil's Wind* where the narration is done in the first person, all the novels of Malgonkar are written from the omniscient point of view. The way Prince Abhayraj in *The Princes* reveals his experiences in the wake of the Instrument of Succession Act and also the mode of first person narrative in *The Devil's Wind* unfold the psychological depths of the protagonists. They become living realities. The author's point of view appears to identify itself with that of the protagonist in these two novels. The first person narrative helps the author achieve a superb integration of the historical material with the fictional mode.

While confronting the problem of conveying "in a language that is not one's own the spirit that is one's own,"[38] Malgonkar shows a commendable care and spontaneity with "the mirror-clear style that gives his fiction its freshness, resonance and individuality."[39] In his narrations, he often resorts to sesquipedalian sentences with a series of words thrown out like pearls. One may quote from *The Princes:*

> The sights and sounds come back to me in sharp jabs, clearing away the mist of the intervening years; the noise of the hooves

pounding on the sawdust-covered ring in an easy rhythm, matching the panting of the shining, sweating horse; the acrid smells of the riding school on a winter's morning, and of refuse being burnt in a nearby incinerator; the grass drenched with dew; the sunlight slanting through the trees in dusty shafts and falling on the white-painted paddock rails; the terrifying jumps built of bamboo and straw. And dominating all, the wiry, bandylegged figure of Hamidulla, the true aristocrat of the ring, praising me and cursing me in hunting field cats and the quaint ring of the orders in an unlearned foreign language. "Fikra-fight! Fikra-fight!" which had nothing to do with fighting but which was Hamidulla's way of saying "Figure of eight."[40]

The language gives an impression of a continuous flow. Marshall Best admires Malgonkar's "lively and colloquial English full of vivid metaphors" which he feels reveals affinities to Conrad and John Masters.[41] Though Malgonkar does not evolve a new idiom like Raja Rao, he injects "vernacular phrase and folk idiom either in English translation or in their raw Indian forms."[42] What interacts a foreign reader in Malgonkar's novels is his abundant references to Indian anecdote in tune with his story-telling technique. For instance, Malgonkar writes of the involvement of Debidayal with Mumtaz.

> Gradually he realised he was no longer a free man, and deep inside himself, he was glad, not sorry. Like the beggar in the fable who had acquired a cat to get rid of the mice in his hut, he had now become involved in the coils of what they called *sansar*—the web of responsibility. You could not keep a cat without providing it with milk: that was the lesson of the fable. You had to keep a cow too, and then a servant to look after the cow, and so on.[43]

Though Malgonkar is not very attentive to the cultural background of certain minor characters and does not try to Indianise their speech-tones by translating the native idioms, he has however shown in his first novel *Distant Drum* the various speech-styles cultivated by different strata ranging from the British Army officer to the betel-chewing politician, Vishnu Saran Dev, evidencing "the accuracy with which these have been observed and recorded."[44] Sometimes Malgonkar achieves the desired effect by deliberate distortions of spellings to reveal the nature of a character:

> "Yaas. The one you put faar regimental ishports and durbars. The new one, naat the old one, ha, ha," said the visitor laughing a knowing laugh. "Will you please have the shamiana shent to the shity haal garden aan the 30th. The Minishter Lala Madhukar is coming to Raniwada, and the District Caangrus committee aaf which I yam the Chairman is giving him a resheption."[45]

Praising Malgonkar's command of English, Mukherjee observes that he has "by-passed the linguistic and stylistic problems inherent in the Indo-Anglian situation."[46] Santa Rama Rau compliments Malgonkar on his "vigorous and dramatic story-telling.[47] Best appreciates Malgonkar's skill "to stretch the reader's willing suspension of disbelief for the sake of a dramatic confrontation.[48] Asnani refers to his dexterity in "creating the authentic atmosphere by weaving the texture of his plot on epic dimensions" and also his "razor-like shrewd and keen observation."[49] At the base of Malgonkar's eventful career as a writer lies his uncanny perception that once you have the story in your grasp "other things shall be added unto it."

In spite of the impressive output of Malgonkar, there have been only two full-length studies devoted to the analysis of his work.[50] A probe into the meaning of his novels revealed through the technique of characterisation with its emphasis on the inner urge for fulfilment deserves critical attention. An attempt is made in the next few pages to examine Malgonkar's *Distant Drum*, *Combat of Shadows*, *The Princes*, *A Bend in the Ganges* and *The Devil's Wind* in the light of this significant theme.

NOTES

1. Khushwant Singh, "Outstanding Books: 1947-77," *The Illustrated Weekly of India* 98.33 14-20 Aug. 1977: 45.

2. Srinivasa Iyengar, *Indian Wring in English* (Bombay: Asia Publishing House, 1973) 423.
3. James Y. Dayananda, *Manohar Malgonkar* (Boston: Twayne Publishers, 1974)23.
4. Henry James, "The Art of Fiction," *American Literature Survey: NationandReligion1860-1900,* ed. MiltonR. Stern and Seymour L. Gross (New Delhi: Light and Life Publishers, 1975) 343.
5. "Author's Note," *Lord Jim* (London: Pan Books Ltd., 1975) 7.
6. Manohar Malgonkar, "Purdah and Caste-marks," *The Times Literary Supplement* 4 June 1964: 491.
7. "Purdah and Caste-marks."
8. Henry James 339.
9. *The Directory of British and American Writers,* 1971.
10. James Y. Dayananda, "On authors and Books: Interview with Manohar Malgonkar," *The Literary Half-Yearly* 16.2 July 1975: 102.
11. Malgonkar, "Purdah and Caste-marks," 491.
12. Walter O'Grady, "On Plot in Modern Fiction: Hardy, James, and Conrad," *Critical Approaches to Fiction,* ed. Shiv K. Kumar and Keith McKean (New York: McGraw-Hill Book Company, 1968) 57-65.
13. Marvin Mudrick, "Character and event in Fiction," *Critical Approaches to Fiction,* 105.
14. The phrase is used by Abhayraj, the narrator in *The Princes* with regard to his father and mother. Malgonkar, *The Princes* (Delhi: Hind Pocket Books, 1970) 235.
15. Henry James 334.
16. D.R. Sharma,"Manohar Malgonkar and the Satpura code," *Quest* March-April 1976: 51-58.
17. Shyam M. Asnani, "A Study of the Novels of Manohar Malgonkar," *The Literary Half-Yearly* 16.2 July 1975: 96.
18. John Cotton, "John Masters," *Contemporary Novelists,* ed. James Vinson (London: St. James Press, 1973) 951.
19. Cotton 852.
20. Dayananda, "On authors and Books: Interview with Manohar Malgonkar," 103.
21. Dayananda 102.
22. Quoted in Marshall A. Best, "Manohar Malgonkar," *Contempo-*

rary Novelists, 825.

23. Malgonkar has published a drama, *Line of Mars* (Delhi: Hind Pocket Books, 1978).
24. *The Ellsworth American* 12 Nov. 1970.
25. Henry James 325.
26. James 325.
27. Dayananda, *Manohar Malgonkar*, 87.
28. Quoted in Best, "Manohar Malgonkar," 851.
29. *The Ellsworth American*.
30. Dayananda, *Manohar Malgonkar*, 88.
31. Dayananda, "Manohar Malgonkar on his novel *The Princes: An Interview*," *Journal of Commonwealth Literature* 9.3:24.
32. Henry James 332.
33. Shakti Batra, "Two Partition Novels," *Indian Literature* July-Sept. 1975: 95.
34. Batra 97.
35. Dayananda, *Manohar Malgonkar*, 150.
36. Dayananda 150.
37. Srinivasa Iyengar 427.
38. Raja Rao, "Foreword," *Kanthapura* (Madras: Oxford Univ. Press, 1947) v.
39. Dayananda, *Manohar Malgonkar*, 125.
40. Malgonkar,*The Princes*, 37.
41. Best, "Manohar Malgonkar," 825.
42. G.S. Amur, *Manohar Malgonkar* (New Delhi: Arnold Heinemann India, 1973) 17-18.
43. Malgonkar, *A Bend in the Ganges* (Delhi: Orient Paperbacks, 1964) 318.
44. Amur 144.
45. Manohar Malgonkar, *Distant Drum* (Delhi: Hind Pocket Books, 1960) 60.
46. Meenakshi Mukherjee, *The Twice-Born Fiction* (New Delhi: Arnold Heinemann India, 1971) 170.
47. Quoted in Asnani 91.
48. Best, "Manohar Malgonkar," 826.
49. Asnani 73.
50. Amur and Dayananda.

Distant Drum

Malgonkar's first novel *Distant Drum* derives from his personal experience as an army officer. He is able to give an inside picture of army life in this novel as he served in the infantry, in counter-intelligence, and on the Army General Staff during World War II as Lieutenant Colonel. He dwells on the thrilling aspects of army life in India at the critical juncture of the Partition days.[1] He has chosen to depict an ardent soldier's fulfilment in living up to the code honoured by the Regimental life.[2] The novel is also an initiation story as it traces the growth of its protagonist Col. Kiran Garud through a variety of his encounters with men and situations.[3] Kiran imbibes the ethos and disciline of the British army and almost becomes "a near symbol of the Satpuras and a vague symbol of the Army itself and its code."[4]

The novel is rendered in two movements—one depicting the present action and the other dealing with the past action in a continual series of flash-back incidents. The first movement covers Kiran's relationship with Bina Sonal, his service at the ridiculously procedure-bound D.W.P. office, and his 'active' service in the Kashmir front which ends up in cease-fire before fire broke out. The second movement gives out a series of incidents like Manners episode, Margot Hedley affair, Kiran's rigorous training at the Dehradun school, the Twin Pagoda Hill attack, the Burma war, the Delhi riots—all reflecting in many ways Kiran's growth as a soldier and his moral maturity. These episodes are a direct transcription of the author's autobiographical experience and Malgonkar evidently feels at home in their presentation through Kiran. Each of these episodes is a well-built anecdote in itself. The brisk nature of the second movement sustains the reader's interest unlike the first one which is somewhat static.[5] The first movement as it is interrupted by a series of flash-back events of the second movement, gets at times disjointed. One may agree with the comment that "where the author has to rely on his invention he is not so happy."[6] Though the events in the second movement are quite in tune with the major theme of Kiran's growth as a soldier, the two movements somehow do not seem to coalesce with each other. Whenever the author attempts the documentation of army life, it tends to be somewhat insipid. This division of interest accounts for many of the novel's weaknesses.[7] Amur accepts that the novel achieves a limited success, but praises it as a technical *tour de force*.[8] Though the novel reveals the author's technical pursuit, it has no such expertise of craftsmanship, a firm design, penetrating characterisation, or a full articulation of a vision that we find in his later fiction.[9]

Though Malgonkar's note of dedication reveals that Duggie Sawhny has cut out two chapters from the book, and Patti Somdutt thinned out the remainder, the first two parts of the novel—'The Regiment' and 'The Staff' still abound in passages and chapters which are not integral to the main story of Kiran's fulfilment as a soldier. The chapters like 'Raniwada Cantonment,' 'Call me KK,' 'It was like leaving Home'—are only a few examples of mere reportage. The novel has however the "prose of an appealing directness and sincerity."[10]

Distant Drum was dismissed as an "unblinking Anglo-philia," a *desi Bhowani Junction*.[11] The comparison with *Bhowani Junction* appears to be not well-founded as it relies heavily on the thin fabric of common historical background. Srinivasa Iyengar is emphatic in his remarks about the comparison:

> Malgonkar is not an indigenous John Masters; nor is *Distant Drum* an Indo-Anglian variation of the Anglo-Indian *Bhowani Junction*. There is, on the contrary, an authentic quality about Malgonkar and his novel that can stand scrutiny without reference to the Masters' recipe.[12]

The experiences of army life depicted in the novel however have a stamp of originality, and warrant no extraneous comparisons. C.L. Proudfoot is right when he praises "the golden thread of authenticity" that runs through the novel "with never a false note."[13] In spite of the stamp of authenticity and its "feeling for form and atmosphere,"[14] *Distant Drum* does not always succeed in realising the characters with force. Kiran alone is a convincing character and others like Bina, Abdul Jamal, Mr.

Sonal, Arun Sanwal, Ropey Booker, Bull Hampton fail to throb with life.

II

The whole interest of the novel centres round the character of Kiran whose quest for fulfilment in his profession imparts to him a measure of nobility and dignity. Kiran looks at his profession not merely as an ambition or "a means of earning a living; it has been rather an end in itself." He discovers his identity as a true soldier committed to his duty unlike his British ideal Ropey Booker who suddenly deserts his profession only to turn into a "box-wallah." Ropey, the soldier-turned-business man, by asking Kiran "to chuck the army" and join his show of the Imperial Metals Company, has "suddenly shrunk" to the normal stature of "a sleek, slightly theatrical civilian" in the eyes of Kiran. Kiran just could not understand the "code" to which Ropey was bound. He could only feel sorry for him:

> Kiran felt sorry for Ropey. Had Ropey lost caste, had he jettisoned his code ? This was not the man he knew, the man who, in his mind, had always represented the ideal of a military commander. He caught himself wishing that Ropey Booker had died in the war, at the height of his glory—while still a colossus. (p. 250)

Kiran would not jettison his code like Ropey. He rejects the tempting offer of Ropey though it would have made him eligible, in the eyes of Mr. Sonal at least, to marry his daughter Bina. He pleads with Ropey:

> We would be failing in our duty to these youngsters and to the future army if we were to quit. Well, it is something like those principles that the Satpuras live by, or try to live upto. No one can explain them, no one can teach them, you have to find them out yourself, by taking out whatever is worthwhile from those who do make an honest effort to live upto them and by testing yourself. It is a sort of debt we have towards those who are now coming. Do you see what I mean, sir? (p. 252)

Ropey fails to appreciate the inexplicable code that the Satpuras live by. Kiran's whole endeavour is to live up to the code. The high-flown lecture on the duty and obligation of a soldier is an indirect reproof of Ropey who failed to fulfil this task. The rigorous training that Kiran received at the Academy was not a waste. It really hardened his spirits and increased his "resistance to stress." As an Indian officer, he could "pick up the sword that Britain has let fall."[15] Kiran has, without knowing, proved true the words of Malcolm Muggeridge that the last true Englishmen are the Indians.[16] Though Kiran appears to be skeptical about his own competence at the start, he emerges as a tough competent battalion commander.

Kiran has won a military cross for his "exemplary devotion to duty in the field of battle." His valour and leadership in the Burma war elevate him to captaincy. Ropey has ordered him to stay back and nurse the wounded. He takes the wounded safely to the other side of the dangerous heights of the Buddha Hill where he successfully meets the machine-gun attack from the Japanese. It was Kiran's first successful attack in which he relished "a heady feeling of unmixed exultation," and nothing else could have given an infantry officer like him the same sense of fulfilment.

> It was the very purpose of existence: the crowning achievement of an infantry officer's life: a successful attack! (p. 161)

Kiran finds his meaning of life in this successful attack. He also has killed a man thrusting his bayonet in hand-to-hand fighting. Though the act is inhuman, Kiran does not feel any sense of guilt. On the other hand, it is for him "a part of fulfilment, a grisly and ghastly detail in the process of learning to become a soldier."

Kiran and his men suffer a crushing defeat, "a crowning indignity," when the Sittang bridge was blown off by the Japanese. But Kiran feels satisfied only when he, along with some of his followers, crosses the bridge again in 1945 exulting as though in "a form of revenge, a fulfilment." (p. 166)

In the Kashmir front, Kiran was to "direct the composite fighting abilities of a thousand men to a single task." But Kiran could not realise his ambition as the war ended up before it began.

Kiran's fulfilment in his duty is not that of a ridiculous "military mind" that goes by hard and fast rules alone. He has his human side in his relationship with his friend Abdul Jamal. He does not want to forego his friendship with Abdul Jamal for ever just because he happened to be in the opposite camp. After the cease-fire, he drinks champagne with his erstwhile colleague Abdul Jamal "under the bushy-topped tree." Although the meeting was purely non-political and sentimental, Kiran had to face the wrath of his higher officials. Brigadier Swarup takes it as "a plain case of conduct unbecoming of an officer." Kiran feels that in the stupid rigidity of the rules, "the very essence of friendship, frankness, had been completely drained off." (p. 241)

> He knew that the Brigadier was finding it unpleasant to have to make a report of such nature against one of his own battalion commanders, and yet his sense of duty combined with the limited vision which is almost the hallmark of the military mind, would not permit him to act otherwise in the matter. (p. 242)

Though Kiran was perfectly convinced in his mind that he had done nothing wrong, it was of no avail to argùe with such "military minds." Friends like Spike Ballur, however, appreciate the good-hearted spirit of Kiran, and try to help him. The matter ends up with a mild warning from General Torgal.

Kiran-Abdul episode proves that true friendship knows no bounds of "narrow, contorted rules" or community hatred. In the Delhi riots when both Hindus and Muslims resort to "ghoulish enormities unknown to primitive men," Kiran and Abdul set out for rescue operations. They save some people from a fire accident and a HIndu woman from being molested by two Muslims. Kiran catches hold of one of the two Muslims and hands over to the police. Later when Kiran enters the mosque where thirty-thousand Muslims were taking refuge, one of the two assailants recognises him and provokes others to kill him. But for the timely protection offered by Abdul, Kiran could have become a scape-goat to the blood-thirstiness of the Muslims. Though Kiran and Abdul belong to the two opposing communities, they work in harmony to establish "a world of new values."

> Neither he nor Abdul had been conscious of the fact that they

belonged to the opposing factions in the riots—that one was a Hindu, the other a Muslim on the verge of setting out for a world of new values. What stood out magnificently secure in that holocaust was the fact that although they belonged to the two opposing communities crazed with vengeance and thirsting for blood, he and Abdul had been able to work together in the closest accord, their loyalties to each other absolutely unruptured by the incessant strain. (pp. 230-31)

Kiran discovers fulfilment in his efforts to build a world of new values. This makes him intensely human, committed to a set of values that foster integrity.

Kiran and Abdul Jamal feel indebted to each other, for each becomes for the other a friend in need. Malgonkar pays considerable attention to depict through their friendship the ideal human relationship. When Abdul Jamal was fatally wounded and left unconscious in the Burma war for the Sittang bridge and the retreat upto Thaungdwingyi, Kiran took his watch, photograph and papers from his wallet to send to his family in the event of Abdul's death. But Abdul survived and later appreciated Kiran as the sole friend who could have conveyed news of his death and his belongings to his family if he died. Again when Kiran was caught up in the scandalous involvement with Margot Medley, Abdul saved Kiran by keeping his name off the picture with his testimony at the court of inquiry about Bob Medley's death.

Kiran's liaison with Margot Medley shows his initiation into sex. She is a "trim, leggy, well-preserved figure" in her mid-thirties. Kiran's association with her starts at Tennis. She provokes him often with her "pair of attractive legs" which play with Kiran's ankle from under the table at the clubs. But when Kiran attempts to kiss her, she "had stopped him and had playfully patted on his cheek instead." During the short respite when he has gone off on a mortar course, his friend Abdul Jamal has "looked after her." Abdul's success makes Kiran mad with desire for her. He seizes the first opportunity to flirt with her, but Margot does not prevent him this time for she considers him "suddenly grown up." They spend "the days of wild rapture, of desire and fulfilment." But the rapture was momentary as Kiran had to go on a long signals course.

The war brings them together in the middle of 1944 when Kiran spends a night with her. He faces an awkward situation as Bob Medley finds him in his green and white fancy pyjamas in his flat. The rumpled bed, the two empty cups of coffee and the bottle of whisky in the room serve as the "objective correlative" of the illegitimate relationship of Kiran and Margot Medley. What would have been one of the common wartime flirtations, however, becomes "a problem of conscience" for Garud.[17] He feels sorry and ashamed of his guilt, and rings up Margot to convey his regrets. Margot accepts the situation quite causally. Kiran reviews the whole situation from Bob Medley's point of view and realises the horror of his sin. He feels

> it was not fair that anyone who had caused the ruin of two lives should get away without any punishment. (p. 35)

Later Kiran comes to know that Bob Medley had blown off his own brains. But for Abdul's false statement at the inquiry that Bob had contemplated suicide long before he went to Calcutta, Kiran would have paid "the price of few moments of rapture."

> He, Kiran Garud, officer and gentleman, had as good as murdered a man, a brother officer, and then had been spared the inevitable retribution, the polite 'request' for his resignation or even a downright dismissal from the service, by the good graces of another. That was the staggering price of what they had learnt to refer to as a 'wartime fling,' the price of few moments of rapture. (p. 39)

Kiran's affair with Margot Medley had graded him down morally, but the saving grace is his repentance for the sin. He later reflects:

> A man could not live without women, true enough; but you had no business to get involved with any particular woman. That much you could guard against. No one could afford two mistakes like that in a life time; no one was going to mess up his life once again. (p. 39)

It is perhaps not to mess up his life once again that Kiran behaves with a good deal of restraint in his behaviour with his beloved Bina Sonal at the critical hour of temptation.

Throughout the novel we find Kiran struggling to find fulfilment both in his duty and in his love for Bina, a strikingly good-looking girl working on the radio. Both his duty and love come in conflict with each other till the last moment when he wins them both because of his restraint and discipline. Kiran discovers that Bina's face has "more distinction than beauty, character more than glamour," and falls terribly in love with her. His confession of love to Bina leaves her distressed because her father wants her to marry a rich gentleman, Arvind Mathur. Kiran tries to console her and shows great restraint and dignity. The lesson he learnt from the Margot Medley affair has stood him in good stead.

The fortitude with which Kiran faces the challenges of life is manifest in his encounter with Mr. Sonal who manoeuvres his transfer tactfully to clear off the way for Bina's marriage with Arvind. Mr. Sonal explains to Kiran why he had to manoeuvre his transfer, and promises to get him back "when things get straightened out." But Kiran refuses this 'kind' gesture.

> "That won't be necessary," Kiran said. "We always finish off our own tigers." (p. 205)

The phrase "we always finish off our own tigers" implies that a person of fortitude (like Kiran) would not yield or succumb to any one but live or die on his own. Mr. Sonal fails to understand his words. The long rejoinder by Kiran makes his stand clear:

> "I am afraid I don't," Kiran said. "But that hardly matters. I see your viewpoint, of course, but not the sense. You want to find a rich husband for your daughter, possibly even against her own feelings in the matter. To ensure that, you are quite determined to go to any length; use all you influence, ruin half-a-dozen careers, if necessary. I am a career officer. To me the army, the profession itself, is a great thing, although in your sense of values it may rank with the lowest forms of life. But I see your point of view, and I am quite prepared to do what you want me to do. And I am prepared to go along with you only for one reason: because I can't afford to risk my professional future; to a career officer like me,

> it is an unfortunate thing to clash with people of your influence. I am ready to give in only because *I want to save something far more personal. My career to me is more important than anything else—more important than your daughter.*" (p. 207, italics mine).

Kiran does not want to relinquish his career as a soldier for the sake of his love. But both the things were important for him. He later feels "as though he had let down both the things he loved above everything: the service and Bina." (p. 208) But he prefers army service. His firm commitment to service prompts Kiran to reject the tempting offer of a job by Ropey Booker, even though it would have made him fit for marriage with Bina. This steadiness of Kiran makes him all the more impressive for Bina. When Kiran meets her after his return from the service at Kashmir, she asks him not to change. She loves him for his integrity. She tells him:

> It is so important for you to be yourself. Don't ever change, please. (p. 259)

Bina knows Kiran's love for her and approves of it. Her earlier doubts whether a man like Kiran could fall in love "really and completely" vanish. Kiran's conflict between love and duty gets resolved. He could win Bina's love without hampering his career in any way. He confides:

> I can never tell you how much I loved you. How much I have missed you . . . these last three months have been torture; it can't tell you how miserable. But please understand. I only wanted to make things easier for you . . . (p. 269)

Bina expresses her readiness to marry him. Kiran reveals to her that he is posted back to Raniwada where he would offer her ideal surroundings, a small bungalow near the bend of the river.

> It is wonderful! In the afternoons, we can have tea on the lawn, just you and me, under the tamarind tree, and *you can see hundreds of parrots and you can hear the buglers practising their calls in the lines, and in the distance, far away, you can hear the drums. . . .* (p. 270) (italics mine)

Kiran's concept of ideal surroundings includes the paraphernalia of a soldier too—the bugles and the drums. The distant drums in the background, signifying his fulfilment as a soldier, add completeness and symphony to his life and love.

Trained under the British regime, Kiran would always try to think out "what a British C.O. would have done in his place," whenever he faced tricky situations. He applies the principles that he inherited from the old army to the changed conditions of modern India, but his is not "a servile, mindless regret for a vanished past."[18] He would not spare even Col. Manners, a shell-shocked commander, for despising the Indian soldiers. He makes an impulsive cry from the other side of the room. When Manners takes objection to this, Kiran seeks permission in quite dignity to leave the mess because the officer seemed to doubt the loyalty of his regiment. Later Manners realises his mistake and expresses regret. This would not make Kiran proud either. He learns to be modest about the incident.

Kiran's uprightness can be seen in his outright refusal to lend the shamiana "for a political show." Lala Vishnu Saran Dev, the Chairman of the District Congress Committee, threatens him in all possible ways:

> I would shay that in refusing this ishmall favour you are running a great rishk. He may complain to your own minshter. You musht remember that thish will amount to belittling a minishter of the gournment aaf which you are only a servant. (pp. 60-61)

But Kiran owes his loyalty only to the regiment and not to any party. He remains unyielding to Lala's threats.

Kiran's single-minded devotion to duty is once again evident as he walks, when his car fails, all the five miles to Palam only to attend to duty the next day. By the time he reached Palam, he had several blisters on his feet and spoiled his much-prided English-made dress shoes. He is not daunted by the discomfort.

Distant Drum defines Kiran's identity as a soldier. Nothing would impede him in the realisation of his goal, neither the lust of Margot Medley nor the genuine love of Bina. He remains unchanged by the pressures brought on him by Mr. Sonal and Lala Vishnu Saran Dev. Ultimately he finds the harmony of his life both in his service and in his love which gracefully merge.

Malgonkar goes further in his next novel *Combat of Shadows* in dealing with the quest for fulfilment on a wider canvas against the backdrop of racial situation in the British India.

NOTES

* Manohar Malgonkar, *Distant Drum* (Delhi: Hind Pocket Books, 1960). All subsequent references with page numbers in parentheses are to this edition.

1. Shyam M. Asnani, "A Study of the novels of Manohar Malgonkar," *The Literary Half-Yearly* 16.2 July 1975: 73.
2. Manohar Malgonkar writes in the prologue to *Distant Drum*: "The book is largely the story of the success or failure of the efforts of one of the officers of the Regiment to live up to its code."
3. James Y. Dayananda, *Manohar Malgonkar* (Boston: Twayne Publishers, 1974) 44; G.S. Amur, *Manohar Malgonkar* (New Delhi: Arnold Heinemann India, 1973) 47.
4. K.R. Srinivasa Iyengar, *Indian Writing in English* (Bombay: Asia Publishing House, 1973) 423.
5. Amur 47 and 52-53.
6. "The Kipling Heritage," *The Times Literary Supplement* 12 May 1961: 289.
7. Amur 56.
8. Amur 57.
9. Dayananda 49.
10. "The Kipling Heritage," 289.
11. See *Shankar's Weekly* 25 June 1961.
12. Srinivasa Iyengar 423.
13. C.L. Proudfoot's letter to Malgonkar, dtd. 1 Nov. 1962. Quoted in Amur 57.
14. Srinivasa Iyengar 425.
15. "The Kipling Heritage," 289.
16. Quoted in Amur 47.
17. Amur 53.
18. "The Kipling Heritage," 289.

Combat of Shadows

*Combat of Shadows** is a sensitive portrayal of an Anglo-Indian girl's search for identity in the rapidly crumbling British India. It is also a saga of "the moral disintegration of a European on foreign soil."[1] Amur praises the skilful treatment of the theme which he believes, compels comparison with Conrad.[2] Malgonkar's narrative technique in this novel shows competence and confident ease. His creative achievement is evident in shaping his personal experiences with the British and the Anglo-Indian into validly realised fiction. Srinivasa Iyengar aptly points out that the novel's success lies in its "careful plotting and the interior stitching" as well as in its capacity "to evoke situations and atmosphere."[3] Asnani finds the interest of the book in "its high-pitched emotional drama which intensifies its narrative interest."[4] Besides its symmetry of form, the poignant human relations depicted in the lives of Henry Winton, Ruby Miranda, and Jean reveal Malgonkar's great depth of understanding.

Combat of Shadows has closer compassion with John Masters's *Bhowani Junction* as it presents the problem of rootlessness confronted by the Anglo-India. Victoria Jones of *Bhowani Junction* is in an unenviable position as she fails to identify herself with the Hindus in spite of her favourable leanings towards them. She is also unable to find a peaceful union with the British. Similarly Ruby Miranda of *Combat of Shadows* gives up her Anglo-Indian lover Eddie Trevor to fulfil her longing to become a *memsahib* in the world of the British. Malgonkar introduces the theme of revenge as Ruby Miranda tries steadfastly to be avenged on Henry Winton for his ruthless betrayal and duplicity.

Ruby's fulfilment through revenge is emphasized as Henry's failure is set off as a foil. Although the novel keeps Henry in full view, he merely provides sharp contrast to the other characters that move in the background with greater energy. Ruby's quest alone gives the thematic unity and coherence to the story which on the surface recounts the many situations to reveal the hopeless futility of Winton.

II

A congenital colour snob, Henry is torn in conflict between "desire and aversion." A man of no integrity, he fails to establish viable relationship either with Ruby Miranda or with his English wife Jean. Even as a young boy he fervently aspired to play rugger for Oxford but the sudden death of his father thwarted him from realising his ambition. His career as a salesman in a firm of second-hand motorcar dealers and as the owner of a used-car business did not fetch him much. He realises that his temperament, upbringing and public school education have not prepared him for "the world of commerce in the cut-throat days of the great depression." He is forced to leave his native land when chance gets him the job of Manager of the Brindian Tea estate on the hills of Assam in India. Chased as he was by failure in life till then, Henry Winton made up his mind to exploit every opportunity to make his career a success. He clings to his profession with remarkable readiness to accommodate his conscience and tries to adapt to the circumstances without scruples. He is certain that "it was dead easy to make a living if you eased up on your sense of values, learned to regard the tenets of the boy-hood code as only a kind of snobbishness—even if you had to get used to a permanent bad taste in your mouth." (p. 56) Henry here is unlike Kiran of *Distant Drum* whose steadfast commitment to profession is matched by his integrity.

Henry is a man of wavering mind with his weakness for women. He loves Ruby Miranda at the first sight, and is equally in love with Jean Walters too. He is also impressed by Gauri, a coolie woman working in his estate. He catches her as she tries to escape with the stolen leaves of tea, but finally lets her go. This act of seeming nobility was merely a camouflage for his inner craving for her. Later when she leads the strike, Henry behaves rudely with her and her brother. His anger, which is disproportionate to the occasion, has its source evidently in his suppressed longing for her. His obsession with status conflicts with his propensity. The dark-skinned Gauri is, of course, unfit to be a mistress for him. He makes a compromise with Anglo-Indian Ruby as he considers her a wee better than the natives.

Henry wavers between Ruby and Jean. When the English woman Jean turns down Henry's proposal of marriage on the pretext that she had a lover, Henry readily goes back to the Anglo-Indian Ruby with his original passion for her. He manages to appoint her as the headmistress of the Silent Hill Primary school taking care of all proprieties.

Henry's selfish irresponsibility is seen in his confrontation with the rogue elephant which has been a menace for many years in the surrounding villages. Lame Kistulal, an aborigin and an expert in tracking down animals, traces the elephant. But Henry fails to shoot the animal as his cartridges prove ineffective. He courts shattering defects and runs away "only vaguely conscious that Kistulal could not run very fast." His irresponsibility costs the life of poor Kistulal. Henry seeks Cockburn's help to save his career. Cockburn cooks up the entire story throwing blame on Kistulal insisting that Kistulal became a sudden victim of the elephant and Henry had tried to rescue him wounding the elephant on the left side. Henry convinces Sudden Dart, the Resident Director of the Company, of the truth of his story and goes scotfree. Kistulal's family is given five hundred rupees and his son Pasupati is employed as a daily-wage coolie by way of compensation.

Put down by the heavy depression caused by the infructuous confrontation with the rogue elephant, Henry seeks his solace in the love of Ruby. He is moved by his lust for her "eyes of the real Chandni-Chowk whore, black and bold." (p. 19) He is a "man of lust without love" seeking sensual fulfilment and paying her a hundred rupees a month of the company's money for his private pleasure. He shudders at the very thought of marrying her because she is not all-white, though he has unwittingly kindled in her the hope of becoming a *memsahib*. Henry treats her merely as an object of pleasure. He continues his sensual relations with her in his gun-room.

When Eddie Trevor applies for the vacancy caused by Jugal Kishore's exit, Henry stoops to suspect that Ruby had advised Eddie to apply for the post so that she could continue her earlier relations with her lover. Henry however wants to be cautious about "the thin line that separates fun from serious involvement" and would use Ruby only for fun. He goes on leave in order to sever his relations with Ruby Miranda once and for all as he fears that his involvement with her might mar his career. The fear prompts him to marry Jean in England.

Ruby's hopes are shattered when Henry brings Jean to India as his wife. She does not however show herself to be a weak woman clinging to him although he has undone her. Henry gets her transferred to the Highlands Club. During the angry confrontation with Henry, Ruby rejects to take even a kiss from him and swears to kill him. Henry also tries to get rid of Eddie Trevor by recommending him for promotion. Suspecting that Pasupati was aware of the secret of Kistulal's death, Henry also gets him transferred to Highlands Club as a gamekeeper. All these timid machinations reveal his base obsession with career.

Eddie Trevor becomes intimate with Jean and excites Henry's jealousy. He suspects that they might be in love. Jean rejects his insinuations and taunts him boldly for his earlier flirtations with Ruby Miranda. Henry bows to her and meekly imposes a new kind of discipline upon himself. He tries to gain her favour by being soft to her to rub off "the dirty spot of his conscience."

Henry's self-discipline gives way when he meets Ruby Miranda at the Highlands Club. Ruby allows him once again to come closer to her. It is a tactful move on her part to give him a long rope to hang himself with. She has nursed her vengeance as a scorned woman and would see his end come what may. Henry asks her foolishly about her engagement with Eddie:

> Ruby turned as though to look at him, peering at his face in the darkness. 'Don't you know?—you, of all people?' she asked. (p. 236)

Ruby's words here carry a subtle meaning that Henry should know that he has broken her innocent love for Eddie by exploiting her craze for *memsahib* status. Henry fails to realise the harm done to her. His monstrous selfishness would not allow him to assess the psychic wound he inflicted on her.

The rogue elephant episode appears to be set down in the structure of the novel with a great deal of symbolic significance. It externalizes the guilt that haunts Henry's conscience. The elephant is the constant reminder of his failure as a hunter. It has become the symbolic Furies that "seek him out and destroy him." In his pursuit of the elephant, he is brought to recognise the hollowness of his cherished illusion that the white skin is superior to the dark in strict adherence to morality. The illusion has long nourished his sense of superiority. Gauri who has known the sting of insult at his hands was a native woman, leads him to the hill-top of Wallach's Folly to witness the clandestine love-making of Jean with Eddie Trevor. Gauri has given him the stunning rebuff by revealing the moral depravity of his *English* wife. Henry is shocked and plans to kill Eddie by a duplicitous device. He lends him his four-sixty-five with spurious cartridges. This causes Eddie's death by the rogue elephant in the forest. Although Henry experiences "the sweet joy of revenge," it costs him Jean's love. She is disgusted with his unmanly machinations and also with his mean trick on Eddie. She has already confessed her love for Eddie. Feeling cheated by his death, she leaves Henry for good. Henry's cup of misery is full with the revelation that Eddie is Sudden Dart's bastard son.

Henry's mind now turns back to Ruby, the only woman who could give him some comfort. This time he thinks of "a purer, nobler, wholly composed image" of Ruby, not that of "a wanton mistress." He makes up his mind to get divorce from Jean and to ask Ruby to be his wife. Henry's change here only reflects the compulsion of the need to have a dependable woman, and Ruby is the only woman left.

Sudden Dart kills the rogue elephant finally and discovers no wounds reportedly caused by Henry earlier in his bid to rescue Kistulal from the charging elephant. It confirms the falsity of Henry's story and also subtly unveils the plan behind Trevor's death. Sudden Dart, Ruby Miranda and Pasupati have now known the man Henry is—a man without honour and without scruples. Dart sends him to the game cottage on the pretext that he should inspect the artificial moon. Ruby is another lure for him to go there. When the contrived fire engulfs him, he suddenly finds the ear-rings returned by Ruby and the empty cartridge. The ladder is cut. He confronts the inevitable fact that his falsity, arrogance and meanness have led him to nemesis.

Henry's failure in life without any sense of fulfilment is in the main due to his inauthenticity or what Sartre calls "bad faith." He has never been able to go beyond the conflicting "desire and aversion in his dealings. He has failed to attain the knowledge of reality. Malgonkar very meaningfully quotes a relevant *sloka* from the *Gita* as an epigraph of the novel."[5]

Amur rightly comments that "the story of Winton's relationship with Ruby is one of betrayal—betrayal of passion through fear."[6] Ever since Sudden Dart's advice, we find Henry obsessed with the fear of losing his career if he had too much involvement with Ruby Miranda. But besides this Henry is just incapable of loving a woman whole-heartedly. His craving either for Ruby or for Jean is merely sensual. A man of guilty conscience, he further entangles himself in the noose of jealousy, suspicion, cowardice and treachery. All these betray his look of integrity and no woman can put up with such a man for long. Ruby and Jean have their own integrity and simply reject Henry. Henry's moral obtuseness thus incapacitates him to realise fulfilment in love. The character of Henry Winton appears to reveal, as Dayananda believes, Malgonkar's preoccupation with the darker side of the nature of the ruling British.[7] However this cannot explain away the careful designing of Henry's life and retribution in the novel, especially in the light of overwhelming evidence for Malgonkar's deep appreciation of the British character in general. Winton's moral depravity should not be interpreted as a criticism of the English as a community. Winton acts out his life as a victim of circumstances, a prisoner of prejudices and finally as a stranger on the foreign soil. He is betrayed "as much by chance and circumstance as by his own defects of character."[8] His failure and fall become all the more tragic against the background of the well-known British integrity.

Among the women characters, Ruby Miranda emerges as the most authentic. She represents "the throbbing, compulsive craving of Anglo-India to seek living kinship with the West." (p. 103) She wants to spare herself the humiliation caused by her penury and her despising social status as an Anglo-Indian in the teeming brown-world of India. So she longs to become "a sahib's lady going into the reserved, all-white clubs with her head held high, escorted by an Englishman without the slightest trace of coloured blood." (p. 103) She does not hesitate to sacrifice her Anglo-Indian lover Eddie Trevor for the fulfilment of this dream.

> No effort was too much for the fulfilment of that constant, aching dream, no sacrifice too great—not even the sacrifice of the love of a man like Eddie Trevor. (p. 103)

When Henry offers her the job as headmistress, she readily goes to join with the intention that she attain the "passport to the dream-world of Eurasian womanhood." Henry loves Ruby, but only to seek animal pleasure. Ruby wants to be his wife and get the rightful status. She craves to lift their relationship from "a hole-and-corner affair of passion to the sphere of love" but in vain. Her frankness is in contrast to the guileful nature of Henry. She even speaks to Henry about her former love for Eddie Trevor.

Ruby's fond dreams are cruelly shattered when Henry returns with Jean, an English woman for his wife. Eddie's forecast that Henry will "have all his fun and then the bugger'll drop you in the muck" is proved true. Henry insults her as "chi-chi street walker" and "half-caste slut." She could not brook the humiliation. She fiercely swears to kill him:

> "I will kill you for this, Henry Winton," she said very coldly, her face looking more like a bloodless papier-mache mask than ever. "No matter how long it takes, I shall kill you for what you have said." (p. 153)

Ruby proves her words true at the end. As a helpless poor woman suddenly abandoned by Henry, Ruby realises that she should pay him in the same coin. During Henry's later visits to the Highlands club, she pretends to be soft to him, pleases him and lures him to the game cottage. She learns to be schematic in order to put down Henry. She would not forgive the soulless cheat who has ruined her life and shattered her dream. She leads Henry to death in the contrived flames at the game cottage where Henry hoped to exploit her once again. She seeks her fulfilment in revenge.

Like Ruby, Jean too is a woman of self-respect and loves integrity in man. Her love for Henry cannot therefore last long. She resents Henry's duplicity and cunningness in concealing his past relations with Ruby. When Henry objects to her intimacy with Eddie Trevor, she hits back at him detailing his past liaison with Ruby. She complains that Henry is still infatuated with Ruby, and says:

> "You have never given me your whole-hearted love, Henry, although you have demanded it from me. You have always held back—and that a woman can never forgive." (p. 200)

She accepts Eddie as her lover to spite the cowardice in Henry. In her transgression, she has expressed her protest without compromise. She makes it clear to Henry that Eddie has replaced him in her affections. Eddie's cold-blooded murder has further revealed to her the impossibility of life with Henry. She is alone. She decides to give up Henry for ever and thus vindicates her faith in integrity.

Jean and Ruby emerge finally as women of independent and stubborn character. They defy falsity in all its manifestations. They refuse to be sold to a life of comfort at the expense of self-respect and independence.

III

The ending of the novel has been often described as melodramatic and much too pat in the nature of poetic justice. One may agree with Asnani for whom the ending is "a serious flaw of the otherwise well-constructed plot."[9]

Amur believes that the final episode of the novel has confused Malgonkar's statement on the racial situation and rendered it less valuable than that of Kipling or Forster.[10] The attitude to racial situation in Kipling and Forster is complex. Forster especially gives it a symbolic function in his *A Passage to India*. Malgonkar does not lead his story to metaphysical frontiers. He appears to be content with a practical narrative pattern rather than symbolic function of the episodes in the story. To interpret *Combat of Shadows* as a valid comment on the racial situation is to put more weight on it than it can possibly bear. In fact the final episode does not confuse the statement on the racial situation. It merely proves that the basic passions of men are the same in spite of their racial differences. Malgonkar works out the theme of revenge as a means of fulfilment and renders the ending somewhat gruesome. The success of the novel rests on the author's dexterous treatment of the theme of fulfilment through revenge that is at the base of all characters in the story. The minor characters bring into focus Ruby's quest for fulfilment through revenge.

Malgonkar moves closer to modern Indian situation in *The*

Princes, as he chooses to depict the disintegration of the Princely India and its endeavour to seek fulfilment in the order already obsolete.

NOTES

* Manohar Malgonkar, *Combat of Shadows* (Delhi: Orient Paperbacks, 1962). All subsequent references with page-numbers in parentheses are to this edition.

1. G.S. Amur, *Manohar Malgonkar* (New Delhi: Arnold Heinemann India, 1973) 76.
2. Amur 76.
3. Srinivasa Iyengar, *Indian Writing in English* (Bombay: Asia Publishing House, 1973) 428.
4. Shyam M. Asnani, "A study of the novels of Manohar Malgonkar," *The Literary Half-Yearly* 16.2 July 1975: 82.
5. "Desire and Aversion are opposite shadows. Those who allow themselves to be overcome by their struggle cannot rise to a knowledge of reality." (From "The Path of Knowledge," *The Bhagavad Gita*)
6. Amur 70.
7. James Y. Dayananda, *Manohar Malgonkar* (Boston: Twayne Publishers, 1974) 55.
8. Srinivasa Iyengar 427.
9. Asnani 81.
10. Amur 76.

The Princes

*The Princes** offers an absorbing account of the princely life in India. It is regarded as the most authentic record of the predicament of the princes, and is probably the most widely-read novel abroad.[1] Grandson of the Prime Minister of a popular Indian state, Malgonkar could observe from inside the princely ways, their vanities and peculiarities. In *The Princes* Malgonkar encounters the problem of fusion of art and history in fiction. The historical consciousness of the novelist, present subtly in his earlier works, comes to the fore in this novel and achieves cohesion with the fictional technique. Malgonkar wants to unfold "the thoughts and ideas of a somewhat tightly-knit social group" the anachronistic world of the princes in India.[2] Malgonkar's knowledge of the real princes is combined with his creative imagination to produce "composite portraits" with a sufficient amount of camouflage.[3] He has chosen "an ordinary educated man," to be the last prince of an imaginary state Begwad which is already in the process of disintegration. Though the major characters of the novel are representative of the class, they emerge in the process as individuals. The novel is not a mere historical record from within but a human exploration of the passions of an extinguishing race.

Comparing *The Princes* with Anand's *Private Life of an Indian Prince,* Saros Cowasjee faults Malgonkar on lacking "distance" in art.[4] He points out:

> A flaw in this novel is that "politics" impinges on "literature"; fidelity to history is achieved at the expense of the story itself, and it is for this reason that the characters, including the narrator whose autobiography this is supposed to be, remain shadowy.[5]

It is difficult to agree with Cowasjee, for in *The Princes* "politics" does not "impinge" but enrich "literature" by giving it a new twist. Cowasjee's view that the historical background in the novel "obtrudes itself upon the development of the narrative or the characters,"[6] is not altogether fair, for history and story never come in conflict in this novel. While Anand subordinates the historical background in his novel to the exposition of the whims and follies of the princes, Malgonkar maintains a balance between the two while recording the princely life with "detachment and wit."[7] He achieves clarity without bitterness and shows the princes as "mixed up human beings just like all of us are."[8] The characters therefore do not tend to be "shadowy or slip-shod." Prince Abhayraj, the narrator-hero, subtly reveals himself while evoking his father's personality vividly through his reminiscences. Ashok Kumar of *The Private Life of an Indian Prince* is passionately in love with Ganga Dasi and goes mad when he loses her. The Maharaja of Begwad in *The Princes* is obsessed with his royal authority and prefers to kill himself before his sceptre is snatched away. Both the characters are intensely human. Yet the latter shows a streak of heroism in his conservatism and is more tragic.[9] Amur justly commends it for being "at once the record of the end of an epoch in Indian history and the story of a man's search for his roots in an age of upheaval and crisis."[10] Both Abhayraj and his father, despite the seeming differences in their outlook, long to preserve their identity and seek fulfilment in the old order.

Malgonkar has nevertheless a clear perception of history in the making. He was a participant-observer like E.M. Forster of a momentous phase in Indian history. *The Princes* could be more appropriately compared with E.M. Forster's *Hill of Devi* for its refreshing historic authenticity. Forster who served in his younger days as a private secretary to H.H. Sir Takoji Rao III of Dewas State Senior, comments that the parallels in *The Princes* and his own experiences are "numerous and heart-rending."[11] William Walsh praises it as "a more perceptive, a more personal and stricken one of the withering of the Princely states."[12] The vivid descriptions of the princes's hypocritical family lives, their concubines, their tiger hunts and their political stunt to preserve their throne even at the cost of national integrity and independence in the novel present an inside view of the princes. Though it reads like a parody, it gives the much-needed documentation of a fascinating piece of social history.[13]

Malgonkar is aware that his faultless history may stand out glaringly defying all attempts at being done into a novel. He has very ably overcome the problem by drawing his characters into the vortex of experience with the agonising quest for fulfilment.

II

Abhayraj in spite of his garb of modernity feels "a purely selfish sense of loss" at the integration of their princely state into the Union. He grows only to assert and idolize the princely instinct of his father. The whipping of Kanakchand, an untouchable who rose to the rank of Minister, at the end of the novel completes the identification between himself and the Maharaja. His father, the Mahraja of Begwad, is an irredeemable autocrat who lives in his own world with a false sense of security. He is confident that "there will always be a Begwad, and there will always be a Bedar ruling it—so long as the sun and the moon go round!" (p. 11) He invites death by the wounded Kolaras giant (tiger) rather than sign the Instrument of merger foregoing his hold over the kingdom. He wants to die before he has lost his identity, as Maharaja. The Maharani seeks her fulfilment in stepping out of falsity that has bound her in the form of royal prestige. She completes the rejection of her former self by eloping with her Muslim lover Abdulla Jan, an ordinary police officer. She does not consider it beneath her dignity either to elope or to change her religion for the sake of her lover. She is the rebellious woman who breaks the shackles of the taboo-ridden love of kings.[14] Abhay, her son, is conscious of the strong urge for fulfilment in both his father and mother. He comments:

> It taught me that my father and mother too were not sinners, but merely helpless human beings caught up in the irresistible urge for fulfilment. (p. 235)

Both Amur and Dayananda point to the dexterous interweaving of the two themes in the novel—the rising freedom struggle and the growing up of a prince.[15] While Dayananda views the novel as an initiation story of the prince, Amur discerns the simultaneity of the epic movement depicting the political unrest from 1938 to 1949 leading to the disintegration of the Princely state of Begwad, and "the development of the protagonist from a state of personal and social alienation caused by emotional problems of childhood and adolescence through a maturing process which involves experience of sex and war to the fulfilment of personality in the realization of human relationships and the affirmation of traditional values."[16] The two movements merge in Abhay's decision to give up his role as an unaffected spectator and to stand by his father.[17] The change is effected very deftly defining the evolution of the prince.

The novel opens with the Maharaja and his son Abhay at loggerheads. The son delights in taunting his father on the latter's proposal of some changes in the constitution to satisfy the Political Department. He knows that it is just an eye-wash measure. The father's sole intention and cherished aim of life is to preserve the integrity of the state at any cost. He says:

> But I would prefer the British to the Gandhites any day, so that the integrity of our state is preserved for all times. It is more important than any thing else—*more important than our own lives, yours and mine.* (p. 16) (italics mine)

The son however doubts openly whether they could separate the destiny of Begwad from the rest of India. The angry father unable to put up with his son's audacity suspects his descent. A cold parting follows after a bitter exchange of words. While the father is exposed as a reactionary, tyrannical and arrogant, the son appears to be a bit more realistic and critical of his father's reckless disregard for the feelings of others. But the core of Abhay's personality reveals the same yearning as that of his father for the old order. The son here takes great pleasure in contradicting the father, thus dramatising his own inner conflict. He comments later:

> I myself went a long way towards sharing his (father's) views and values as far as our state was concerned. Indeed it seems to me that with the passing of the years, *I have come to identify myself more and more with those values*, with the result that today *I feel myself a spokesman for whatever the princely order once stood for.* (p.

18) (italics mine)

The son has finally come full circle in identifying himself with his father and the old order he has all along represented.

Abhay reveals at length how the reality negates his father's hopes of false security. The state of Begwad was merged with the vast totality of India within ten years of their argument and the prince had to sign the "doleful document," the Instrument of merger surrendering all his powers as the ruler.

The novel is concerned with the evolution of Abhay as he is exposed to the conflicting loyalties and ideologies. His attitude towards his father from his childhood had been one of love and hate. Though the dominant urge of his childhood was to prove his devotion to his father, he had also felt strong antipathy. When his pet ram "cannonball" was killed in the cruel ram fight, the grief-stricken prince wanted to put an end to his father. The experience turns out to be a powerful factor in his initiation. The Maharaja admonishes him:

> It is most important not to squeal, to show hurt. Be a man, my son. There is a great English poem you must read sometime. Ask Mr. Moreton to show it to you. "Make me a Man, O Lord." It is a great thing to be a man . . . a true man. Tears are the refuge of the weak. Will you promise me that you will never break down; at least when you are not by yourself ? (p. 31)

The innocent boy was made to eat the eyes of his own pet ram with great difficulty and also finally with "a surge of triumph."

Abhay as a boy is innocent and considerate. When Kanakchand, an untouchable, has lost his books in his fight with Charudatt, the prince comes to his rescue by providing him with his own. Moreton, his tutor appreciates this generous gesture of the prince:

> It is one of the most satisfying things in life to be able to give someone what he really needs; only it takes a long, long time for most of us to find it out. (p. 45)

Abhay is moved when he comes into "direct contact with the quivering poverty of India" in Kanakchand. He even writes an essay in English for Kanakchand to enable the latter to get a scholarship. But the things go wrong. Kanakchand is flogged in public by the Maharaja for cheating and also for possessing the banned Gandhi cap. The tender prince feels anguished for Kanakchand and hates his father for his cruel, inhuman act. Though Abhay's mother finances Kanakchand's education, the incident of flogging impairs their relationship.

The prince as a boy was exposed to the influence of his parents: father who was cruel and mother who was tender. While he hated the cruelty of his father, he was also enchanted by his majesty. While at college, he is acutely distressed:

> For the first few days I was lonely and homesick, and, oddly enough, I seemed to miss my father most. Although he represented all the authority, the sternness, the discipline I had encountered in my life, he was also someone I had always striven to live up to. And I missed my mother too, for she had been the source of all the kindness and love and laughter and lightness that had come to my share. I vowed that I would never allow myself to be separated from the watch she had given me, and I also made a resolve not to grow up to be cruel and to develop tolerance. (p. 75)

Above all, the charm of the royal grandeur fascinates him very much. He begins to cherish the prestige with an element of pride. He even bullies Abdulla Jan, the police officer, for having used his gun during his absence. The question of honour is associated with his instinctive savagery. He reflects:

> Perhaps I would have used it (the gun) if I had killed Abdulla Jan with it, for his blood would have purified it. I shuddered. Where had I heard that blood could purify? Was it some voice from the past, leading me back to the days of human sacrifices? The sort of thing which had provoked the first Abhayraj into cutting off the head of his victims and decorating the walls of his fort? (p. 83)

The prince is conscious of his own savage instinct and feels ashamed of it. These sentiments do not last long. We find him more and more like his father and forefathers as he grows.

Even the prince's inclination to join the war is in keeping with the spirit of kings. Though his father is convinced that there is no need for Abhay to fight against the Germans, he feels proud of his son's instinct to join the war. The Maharaja exults that the Bedars have always been soldiers and therefore could never be kept out of war.

During his visit to Patalpet, the secret treasure of the Bedars, the son comes closer to his father and experiences the feeling of being "a man who was beginning to understand the sort of values that obsessed his father." (p. 95) The visit symbolises the affinity that binds the prince and his father in the convention that lends meaning to their life. The prince picks up a special duelling pistol from the treasure. The pistol is one of the pair, the twin of which was earlier picked up by the Maharaja. He has the same propensities as his father. Malgonkar says that he had deliberately made the father and son resemble each other to add "a sense of drama," by the Patalpet visit:

> . . . they had so much and their needs were also so much, at the same time, psychologically, they were upset by the same sort of things, they had the same inhibitions, they seemed to have the same lusts, roughly the same mental processes and I wanted to identify this affinity between the father and son, and I thought I could not do it better than by the emphatic means of their independently going into this place where they could have chosen anything at all and they both came out with what they fancy, the best thing of all, the pistol.[18]

The affinity is further emphasised by a series of incidents culminating in the final episode of flogging.

Three weeks before the Independence day, the princes were called upon to sign the Instrument of Accession handing over to the Government control only of defence, foreign affairs and communications wihin their states. For the Maharaja, it was the most sorrowful event of his life. The prince comments:

> I was aware that I was in the presence of sorrow; a grief deeper than when his brother died, a humiliation far more wounding than when his Maharani had taken a lover. (p. 265)

The Maharaja appears to be quite heroic even when the roots of his authenticity are shaken. Though the power is wrested from him, he proudly repeats the line from the *Bhagavad Gita.*

> I am rich and well-born; who else is equal to me? I will sacrifice, I will give; in that I shall rejoice. (p. 300)

When the *Praja Mandal* occupy the king's administrative building and hoist their flag, the king ventures to go into the gathering to reinstate his own flag. He evinces an extraordinary courage here. There is also something heroic about his death. Intending to set a record by killing his hundredth tiger in his fiftieth year, he could only wound the biggest Kolaras tiger. He follows the wounded tiger all alone knowing that this would mean death. The tiger mauls him to death. The intrepid act proves the never-drooping spirit of the king. He hates the misery of signing the impending Instrument of merger and welcomes death which he prefers to the abdication of power.

Prince Abhayraj becomes the ruler of Begwad exactly for forty-nine days.[19] It is quite ironical that Abhay begins to identify himself with the old order just when it is set on disintegration wrought by the inexorable forces of historical inevitability.

The novel ends with the whipping scene of Kanakchand in public. Kanakchand, the Education Minister, is present to rename Ashokraj High School as the New National High School. He reveals that it was the place where he was flogged as a boy for no reason. The prince furiously objects to the speech and whips him on the dais with his riding crop as his father had done earlier.

> I saw him close, staring at me in utter disbelief, insolent no longer but cowering, shrinking, frightened; the face of a schoolboy in the grip of terror. I raised the crop high. I brought it down.
>
> "This I have sworn," I was muttering to myself. *"This have I fulfilled."* (pp. 342-43) (italics mine)

This revenge is also a trait of the royal instinct. With this act of revenge, the process of his identification with the old order becomes complete.

Malgonkar says that the repetition of the whipping scene at the end is the novelist's trick not only to show identity but also "to dramatize a situation a little bit."[20] The dramatizing here, it should be remarked, is a major flaw and it undermines the structure of the novel as a whole. The writer reveals his unabashed partiality towards the royalty as he distorts Kanakchand's character quite deliberately bordering on irresponsibility. The whipping scene at the close of the novel should be viewed as a serious blemish as it demands suspension of disbelief to an incredible extent with its strange suggestion that a fallen prince could flog a minister and yet go scotfree for the simple reason that the latter happens to be a Harijan. Even if the last scene is interpreted as completing the process of protagonist's identification with the crumbling old order and also as a triumphant proof of fulfilment, it remains unrealised and floats about menacingly. Naipaul hits out at the conclusion in disconcerting terms:

> This is the action with which the book ends. This is what is presented for our approval; this is what after the tragedy of the Prince's fall, restores calm of mind to the narrator and is meant to restore it to us.[21]

The episode is for him an unmistakable proof of "withdrawal, denial, confusion of values" which characterize the novel.[22]

III

Apart from the picturesque delineation of the prince, the novel can also be studied as an interesting treatise on the feudal attitude to love. The prince falls in love with Minnie. He is initiated into the "searching, revealing, intimate experience" of sex. The Maharaja would allow her to be his son's mistress but not his wife. But the prince's attitude to love is just in tune with that of the old order which the maharaja represents. For Abhay, Minnie is an object of lust and not of love. His approach is cold and business-like. It is evident in the last love scene between them. When Minnie voluntarily submits herself to him, he mistakes it for a business deal. The sheer inability of the prince to fathom the feelings of Minnie compels her to desert him.

The prince marries Kamala, the eldest daughter of the Raja of

Akheti as arranged by his father. It was sheerly "a marriage of convenience" and a social obligation to provide a Maharani for the kingdom. The prince confesses that there is not even a single spark of love in him for Kamala. He continues his illicit contacts with Zarina, the concubine pampered for him. This of course provides him with one more conventional attribute of a prince. Wife or concubine has no place in his heart.

The subject of love is a taboo for the princes. The Maharaja considers love as a duty or social obligation. He lectures slovenly on marriage:

> a marriage is a sacred thing. It is not a private, purely personal matter at all, but an affair of state, as it were. Even the Political Department has an interest. There is a duty, an obligation, to marry someone suitable. Someone whom the people will one day have to accept as their Maharani. (p. 166)

These words have a ring of pomposity in the mouth of the Maharaja who has ill-treated his wife as an untouchable. He regarded her as "a woman with a white foot," bringing bad luck wherever she went. The queen speaks of her marriage very pathetically as "being tied to a pair of feet." She relates to her son the sad story of her being kicked on the very first night of their marriage by her husband. She was discarded by her husband and "left alone like a leper." She had to suppress her instinct "to live the life of a normal woman." The prince at first pities her predicament and advises her to "break away before it is too late."

> "Maji," I said. "Go away from here. Go somewhere and live life of your own. You have your own money, your own houses. You can't go on living here, the way you are living; shut away forgotten. I have always pitied you, felt for you . . ." (p. 164)

When she finally decides to go, the son fails to appreciate the spirit of her action. She comes to inform him of her departure to Karachi along with Abdulla Jan. The prince insults her very cruelly. But the rebellious mother retorts:

> I may be a bitch but I am no longer a shameless woman of the

> streets. I was one, all these years when I lived with a man in sin, But remember I had been abandoned by my husband—I was a discarded woman (p. 319)

The prince feels mortified when she exposes the sham and hypocrisy of the king's love like an iconoclast.

> It was—it was like being an animal, a leper kept in segregation until I went away, preferring to be a woman of the streets, as you have said, to being a Maharani in darkness... never knowing what it was to be a complete woman. (p. 320)

The Maharani prefers the state of a "a woman of the streets" to the status of "a Maharani in darkness." She seeks fulfilment in being "a complete woman" who could secure the love and affection of her husband. Her confrontation with Abhay proves the fact that in spite of her best efforts to change him, he has always been his (the Maharaja's) boy.

IV

Naipaul compliments *The Princes* on its honesty.[23] Nevertheless, he finds fault with Malgonkar's failure to confront the *quivering* poverty of India. He charges that "all the cruelty of India is magicked away in text book western phrases" in the novel.[24] The withdrawal of Malgonker may be due to his refusal to deal with what is unfamiliar to him, though this would not absolve him as an imaginative writer. However the novel succeeds in revealing the agonising poverty and haplessness of Indian masses indirectly through the callousness, lethargy and in-humanity of the rulers who play out the tragi-comedy of life at a high cost.

The structure of the novel has received a great deal of explication, especially in the hands of Dayananda. He has shown very ably the functional aspects of the rhythms of phrases, characters, incidents and symbols as being integral to the novel.[25] The dying tiger, a species in the process of extinction, symbolizes the fading princely order. It may also leave a silent comment on the dignity in dissolution, a sort of "grace under pressure" as shown in the death of the Maharaja.

The Princes is a creditable endeavour to illustrate the theme of fulfilment in various forms that make life tragic and human Marshall A. Best has rightly called it "the most thoughtful, and perhaps most distinguished work."[26]

In his next novel *A Bend in the Ganges,* Malgonkar delineates the theme of fulfilment in love on an ideological plane. The novel deals with the last few turbulent years before India became independent.

NOTES

* Manohar Malgonkar, *The Princes* (Delhi: Hind Pocket Books, 1970). All subsequent references with page numbers in parentheses are to this edition.

1. James Y. Dayananda, "Manohar Malgonkar on his novel *The Princes:* An Interview," *Journal of Commonwealth Literature* 9.3:21-28.
2. "Author's Note," *The Princes*, 7
3. Dayananda 24.
4. Saros Cowasjee, "The Princes in Indian Fiction," *Kakatiya Journal of English Studies* 2.1 Spring 1977:65.
5. Saros Cowasjee 62.
6. Cowasjee 64.
7. "The Ruling Passions," *The Times Literary Supplement* 21 June 1963:457.
8. Dayananda 26.
9. Cf. G..J. Chinneswararao, "Anand's *Private Life* and Malgonkar's *The Princes,*" *The Journal of Indian Writing in English* 4.1 Jan 1976: 15-21.
10. G.S. Amur *Manohar Malgonkar* (New Delhi: Arnold Heinemann India, 1973) 78.
11. Quoted in James Y. Dayananda, "On Authors and Books: An Interview with Manohar Malgonkar," *The Literary Half-Yearly* 16.2 July 1975:99.

12. William Walsh, "Nataraja and the Packet of Saffron: The Indian Novel in English," *Readings in Commonwealth Literature* (London: Clarendon Press, 1973) 51-57.
13. "Ruling Passions," 457.
14. Cf. I. Jayashri "Women versus Tradition in the Novels of Manohar Malgonkar," *Triveni* 45.2 July-Sept. 1976: 73-80.
15. Amur 80-81; and James Y. Dayananda, *Manohar Malgonkar* (Boston: Twayne Publishers, 1974) 90.
16. Amur 80.
17. Amur 81.
18. Dayananda, "Manohar Malgonkar on his novel *The Princes:* An Interview," 26.
19. It is quite interesting to note that Malgonkar wrote this novel exactly in forty-nine days. He says: "I wrote it in forty nine days and to bring that forty—nine days into the book, I made my maharajah go through forty-nine days, just to sort of pinpoint the number." Dayananda 22.
20. Dayananda 26.
21. V.S. Naipaul, *An Area of Darkness* (England: Penguin Books, 1975) 66.
22. Naipaul 62.
23. Naipaul 62.
24. Naipaul 67.
25. James Y. Dayananda, "Rhythm in Manohar Malgonkar's *The Princes,*" *Literature East and West* 15.1 March 1971:55-73.
26. Marshall A. Best, "Manohar Malgonkar," *Contemporary Novelists*, ed. James Vinson (London: St. James Press, 1973) 826.

A Bend in the Ganges

*A Bend in the Ganges** which E.M. Forster chose as the best book of the year (1964), stands out as an example of Malgonkar's insight into life. In this novel Malgonkar introduces a domestic tale of two characters against the background of the tense years of the freedom struggle. Like Khushwant Singh's *A Train to Pakistan*, Malgonkar's novel is exact about events in relation to time and close to the facts. While graphically depicting the horror and futility of the Partition riots, Malgonkar gains in depth by probing the validity of ideologies of violence and nonviolence and their relevance to life. The novel almost approaches the epic movement in its authentic evaluation of human tragedy. Both Gian and Debidayal espouse non-violence and violence as definite ways of life, and yet finally in their confrontation with the inevitable reality of life they realise the futility of the abstract formulations. Both seek and find real fulfilment in the humanizing power of love.

Malgonkar attempts to pinpoint in the novel the inadmissibility of any ideology being valid for the many unpredictable and inexplicable situations of life. Ideologies divorced from the reality of life become sterile and anti-human. Life in the rich variety refuses to be moulded into a neat framework of a given ideology. Mahatma Gandhi himself was in doubt about his experiment with the ideology of non-violence. Malgonkar quotes the passage as the epigraph of his novel:

> It almost appears as if we are nursing in our bosoms the desire to take revenge the first time we get the opportunity. Can true, voluntary non-violence come out of this seeming forced non-violence of the week? Is it not a futile experiment I am conducting? What if, when the fury bursts, not a man, woman, or child is safe and every man's hand is raised against his neighbour?

Gandhi's own fears came true in the wake of the Independence, revealing the incongruity of non-violence juxtaposed to the grim holocaust.

> What was achieved through non-violence brought with it one of the bloodiest upheavals of history: twelve million people had to flee, leaving their homes nearly half a million were killed; over a hundred thousand women, young and old, were abducted, raped, mutilated.[1]

One may in fact agree with Tekchand in the novel that for the bulk of the people, Gandhi's message of non-violence had no other significance than as a mere political expedient:

> It seemed that the moment the grip of British power was loosened, the population of the subcontinent had discarded non-violence overnight and were now spending themselves on orgies of violence which seemed *to fulfil some basic urge.* (p. 333) (italics mine)

Malgonkar also depicts man's inner urge for violence or his "hidden capacity for violence often brought out by the destructive acts of others."[2] Perhaps Malgonkar would like to ask more precisely like the revolutionary Basu in the novel:

> Would you remain non-violent if someone threw acid at the girl you loved? Would Gandhi? (p. 291)

Malgonkar appears to discredit non-violence through the weak and fumbling Gian even before the terms are stated properly. Amur accuses Malgonkar of ignoring the non-violence of the strong which demands "a greater heroism than violence itself" as exemplified by the Mahatma and Martin Luther King in their lives.[3] Malgonkar gives the impression that he wants to tell the whole story from the point of view of revolutionaries who condemn non-violence as "the philosophy of sheep."[4] Both Amur and Asnani accuse him of "being biased and influenced by his own personal predilections" in focusing only on the superficial aspect of non-violence.[5]

It is true that non-violence demands greater courage then violence. But in practice it has become a creed of hypocrisy. Very few among the throng who swear by non-violence measure up to the high standard of integrity and discipline demanded of it. Malgonker may have deliberately shaped Gian in order to reveal with pitiless irony the gap between precept and practice. He has very cautiously stayed away from the easy temptation of fashioning Gian into an inviolable champion of non-violence.

He would have in all probability created a blood-less saint. It is difficult to test non-violence in a realistic situation with credibility. Often the idealistic heroes tend to be sentimental in fiction. In the present context ideals can be affirmed only by the technique of indirection or what Ihab Hassan chooses to call "deflection." Hassan believes that there is a persistent ironic view of values in the recent fiction. Therefore "the only way to pray is to blaspheme" and the only way to celebrate is to denigrate ironically.[6] Gian's character illustrates the technique of indirection in revealing the strength of non-violence through caricature or deflection.

Malgonkar does not, however, uphold violence as a way of life. In the death of Debidayal, Malgonkar discards violence by revealing its self-consuming nature. Ultimately the affirmation is in "the value of love which transcends violence and non-violence—the real and the unreal—and brings about freedom and fulfilment to the individuals."[7] Both Gian and Debidayal seek their redemption in love.

Although *A Bend in the Ganges* like *A Train to Pakistan* affirms the value of love as transcending all barriers against the background of horrid communal riots, Malgonkar's novel examines more thoroughly the steady though subtle corruption of the idealist freedom fighters in the context of communal loyalties. The novel also draws comparison with John Masters's *Bhowani Junction* in the authentic description of the historic background of the freedom struggle.

Malgonkar evokes vividly the rural atmosphere of Konshet. His descriptions of the "rust-coloured bullocks Raja and Sarja," the cartman Tukaram and Aji, the cause of the domestic feud between the 'Big House' and the 'Little House'—evoke the spirit of village life without a touch of simplistic sentimentality. His depiction of Jaora feast and the naked dance of the Jaoras provides the weird and primitive urge for life and continuity as a contrast to the life-negating violence. It is integral to the structure of the novel, and not superficial as Robin White believes. It may be true that the novel is somewhat sprawling and shows gusto for "too many episodes and too many stories."[9] Yet it succeeds in creating the sweep of the historic forces marching inexorably. Malgonkar felt that he could have "cut down about 30,000 words from it and made perhaps a better book of it.[10] But the process would have impaired the force that has characterized it. It is argued that dispensing with episodes such as the undressing scene in the chapter "Only in Pearls" or Gian's audacious retreat by swimming across the river at Birchi-bagh in the second chapter, the novel could gain in compactness. But the feel of serenity of life evoked by the undressing scene acts as a necessary contrast to the demonic violence that was to erupt a little later in the story.

II

A Bend in the Ganges is concerned with the theme of individual's quest for fulfilment in moral identity. The terms are specified in the structure of the novel which almost borders on "political and philosophical allegory."[11] Gian and Debidayal represent two different ideologies of life. Gian accepts the path of non-violence and truth, and in his interaction with a crucial event in life jettisons his principles. He kills Vishnu Dutt, the murderer of his brother. The murder changes his life and principles totally. While on deportation in the Andamans and subsequently outside the jail he leads a cunning and deceitful life full of lies to get himself to a comfortabe position. Towards the end he affirms the meaning of his life through an act of unselfish love born of deep understanding.

Debidayal chooses the path of violence. He is betrayed by his friend and freedom fighter Shafi Usman. He undergoes suffering and humiliation at the hands of the British authorities in the Andamans, collaborates with the Japanese and comes back to India. His compassion for Mumtaz transforms him and compels him to review the philosophy of his life. Both Gian and Debidayal with their contrasting natures and conflicting ways come to realise the same redeeming factor—affirmation through love.[12] In the course of events, Gian survives and continues to grow while Debidayal becomes a victim of the Hindu-Muslim riots. Dayananda perceptively comments that Gian is the initiation hero who grows through his diverse experiences in many areas; "his formal schooling, religion, sex, marriage, work, social relationship, and travel," while Debidayal and Shafi Usman fail to confront life in its completeness.[13]

Malgonkar introduces several characters like Sundari, Gopal, Tekchand, Aji, Hari, Basu, and Patrick Mulligan to reveal the richness of life from many points of view and provides viable background for the violent action of the novel. He makes his characters realistic and complex. They cannot be drawn into neat categorisation of good and bad.

The interest of the novel centres round the vigorous characterisation but not in the dramatic effect created by the author. Malgonkar's characters have the force of life, and it is unjust to discount them as "sketchy and confused."[14] They represent the complexity of life, and compel the reader's attention with their intense quest for identity or self-discovery.

Gian is a man of conflict. He is aware of his weaknesses and struggles to seek fulfilment in life. At the beginning of the novel, Gian is presented as an impulsive and sudden convert to Gandhism and accepts the call for boycotting the British goods. Gian steps out from the crowd, makes a bonfire of his dark-blue and yellow football blazer, his most prized possession. HIs conversion was not based on personal conviction and adult understanding. At the house of Debidayal, he fails to defend his choice. He feels perturbed and infirm. He begins to doubt whether it was "merely a moment of weakness" or "the sight of a beautiful woman throwing away her fur coat into a fire" (p. 18) that prompted him to make his choice. He was perhaps governed by vanity.

In the domestic feud between the "Big House" and the "Little House" over Piploda, a piece of scrub and jungle, Hari his brother boldly faces the challenge of Vishnu Dutt and his men. Though Gian reminds himself time and again that his non-violence is of the strong "arising from courage, not cowardice," he feels "weak and trembling." He recognises "the cold hard pebble of fear" within himself.

> He wished to hang back, to run away, to leave this evil place and never to see it again. This was not his fight; it was Hari's, their

father's grandfather Dada's. (p. 48)

Evidently his thoughts point to his cowardice and he fails to discharge his duty at a crucial moment when Vishun Dutt murders Hari. Later Gian becomes conscious of his cowardice and questions himself:

> Was that why he had embraced the philosophy of non-violence without question—from physical cowardice, not from courage. Was his non-violence merely that of the rabbit refusing to confront the hound? (p. 50)

Gian's growth begins with his shedding the principle of non-violence as a way of life. He seems to debate that it was a political expedient in the struggle against the British. It could not serve as a philosophy of life itself. He gets deflated by his collisions with reality. His fall from non-violence is quick and headlong. He kills Vishnu Dutt with the same axe with which Vishnu Dutt killed his brother.

Gian's life in the Andamans and later in India is "a bundle of lies and series of deceitful deeds."[15] Gian is conscious that his non-violence had deserted him the moment it met a major test, and he fears that even his nationalism has become somewhat infirm gradually through his contact with the British officials of "sterling character." He regrets that he could not hold on to his beliefs with "unswerving rigidity" like Debidayal. He appears to be "typical of the youth of India, vacillating, always seeking new anchors, new directions. devoid of any basic convictions." (p. 155) Gian had already jettisoned non-violence, and he is not sure that he would go a long way with truth. His only ambition of life now is to become a *feri* and settle comfortably in the Andamans. Gian gains the favours of Mulligan with his obsequious tactics and earns a paid job as well. He also acts as "an administrative spy" for Mulligan over Debidayal and other prisoners. When Debidayal tries to escape, Gian blows the secret whistle and becomes responsible for getting Debi flogged. All the prisoners detest and ostracise him. However, he feels sorry for his impulsive action and tries to make amends for it by offering help to Debi to escape according to the big Ramoshi's plans. But Debi outrightly rejects his plans and damns him:

> I would willingly rot in a cell here rather than associate with

someone like you and become free. You are scum; you are far worse than Balbahadur because he at least is openly hostile—you spout truth and non-violence; you are the sort of man through whom men like Mulligan rule our country, keep us enslaved; you are a slave working for the masters, proud of the service he renders, hankering after the rewards. (p. 198)

Gian's abysmal moral debasement can be seen in his act of cutting through the neck of the big Ramoshi Ghasita's corpse to get the gold sovereigns from his "Khobri" without any scruples. When the Japanese seize the Andamans, he escapes to India with the help of Mulligan.

In India Gian begins his search for new identity to conceal the past. He becomes Maruti Rao for some time and lives on the gold sovereigns. He is now conscious that his prison-life has left him only "a legacy of shame to carry through life." On the pretext of selling the idol of Shiva, Gian goes to Tekchand, exploits his distress and anxiety for his son Debidayal and gets a job in the Kerwad construction company in Bombay. Nevertheless, he feels oppressed and debased and wants to be free from his humiliating obligations to Debidayal's family. He decides to lead a life a "faceless anonymity" in hibernation for some time.

Sundari gets attracted to him, and Gian too feels "a sense of contentment he had not imagined possible" in her association though hip longing for her bore "strong overtones of sensuality." During the bombardment of the Docks, Sundari rescues him and they become more intimate. They plunge into "unrestrained sexual intimacy." He yearns to open his heart to her and tells her that he has loved her. But the thought that his romance is based on deceit torments him. He has to cast away his false self in order to affirm his love.

Sundari rejects Gian with great contempt as she learns his perfidy to Debidayal in the Andamans. She calls him a "male-whore" and insults his love. She says:

Love! How grotesque the word sounds in the mouth of someone like you . . ., an insult to the kind of love that even a woman in a whore-house can achieve. Love for what? My father's money? You thought his son would never come back. (p. 330)

Gian feels abashed and tries to defend himself saying:

> I had just begun to believe in myself, taking courage in the fact that somewhere, *in spite of all his weaknesses, there is in every man some thing that he can value.* You have now destroyed that faith. (p. 330) (italics mine)

Perhaps that "something" he valued is his genuine feeling of love for her. He vindicates it when he goes to Duriabad to rescue Sundari, Tekchand and his wife held up in the riots. When Sundari accuses him of some "selfish motive" and discounts his love, he is able to face her with resolution. He tells her:

> 'Since we are talking about my degradation, may I tell you that that is partly the reason why I have come?' Gian said. 'To try and prove, if only to myself, that there can be some good in the weakest of human beings . . . don't you see that I am trying to make up'? (pp. 351-52)

The pure and unselfish love turns the weak personality of Gian into a strong one and provides him moral identity. His complacent smile, assurance, and "the arrogant awareness of being in command" almost shake Sundari with anger. Gian stays on in their house and tries to rescue them from Shafi who comes to attack them. In the scuffle, Sundari's mother is killed and Sundari kills Shafi with the idol of Shiva. Fortunately they join the convoy and Gian escorts them. Ironically the novel ends with Patrick Mulligan commanding Gian to move forward in the convoy. This is, however, no reflection on the character of Gian. It is "symbolic" of how English colonialism stood behind the terrible bloodshed of Partition.[16]

As Amur points out, "the Gian who survived is not the Gian who built his life on falsehood, but a morally regenerated individual."[17] It is only by immersion in the flux of experience—in Konshet, in the Andamans and in Duriabad—that he achieves authenticity.[18] He evolves through experience and suffering. It is difficult to agree with S.C. Sood that Gian "hardly grows" and the novel exposes only his "duality."[19] What Malgonkar wants to suggest is the possibility of regeneration even in the weakest of human being. It is true that Gian is duplicitous but his rescue of Sundari and others at the risk of his life is no mean achievement. Gian is here led by a self-less love for Sundari. In fact Gian's growth is more spectacular than that of Debidayal. Both of them shed their ideologies and seek ultimate fulfilment in the overpowering value of love. Gian and Debidayal serve as the instruments of the theme of fulfilment. Hence Sood's argument Debidayal alone qualifies to be the hero of the novel fails to convince.

Malgonkar builds up Debidayal as a parallel to Gian. The interest of the novel is evoked by this parallelism of the contrasting characters. Debidayal emerges as a satisfying symbol of violence. Though born of wealthy parents, he opts out of the easy way of life to become a fierce revolutionary. The attempted molestation of his mother by a British soldier pushes him to the path of violence. He joins the group of "angry young men" called the freedom fighters under the leadership of Shafi and readily helps them by supplying the explosives, "the life-blood of any terrorist movement." He seeks fulfilment in terrorist activities. When he sets the British jet plane on fire, his face assumes "an almost frightening malevolence, as though he were gripped by the joy of some secret fulfilment much greater than the mere burning of a plane." (p. 82)

Even in the Andamans his spirits do not droop. He refuses to *salaam* his British masters in the jail. His nationalism is firm unlike that of Gian. As the author comments:

> All he wanted was to go back and finish his interrupted work until the sunrise of their freedom, as Shafi had described it that day; to join hands with the others in the ceaseless fight against the Raaj. . . . (pp. 159-60)

His bid to escape from the prison fails and he is punished with flogging. But it raises him to a heroic stature in the eyes of the fellow convicts. He comes back to India to act as an agent for the Japanese and to prepare grounds for the Japanese march to India. Although he looks to the future under the Japanese, he sadly realises that the Japanese "were ruthless, overbearing, and cruel—far more cruel than the British could ever be."

In India he joins a Tea company in Assam as Kaluram and leads a passive life withdrawn from politics. He is conscious of a deep change in his attitude:

> He wondered whether all the exposure to what Gandhi had

> described as man's inhumanity to man had converted him to his doctrine of non-violence? Or was it just his feeling of repulsion against his fellow-Indians, men like Shafi the Brigadier and Gian Talwar, that had made his spirit curdle? (p. 268)

He has travelled from violence to love through non-violence. His mode of revenge upon Shafi is somewhat intriguing. He spites Shafi by buying from the brothel Shafi's girl Mumtaz. When Shafi throws an acid bulb at her, he rescues her at great risk to his life.

Gradually Debi gets entangled in the coils of *sansar* with Mumtaz as their relationship of the master and the slave changes into that of man and wife. The stress of circumstances and the personal experience of the great humanising force in the innocent love of Mumtaz transform him. Finally Debidayal seeks his refuge in love like Gian. While his death by violence in the communal riots and his refuge in the innocent love coalesce in his consciousness, the episode provides a telling comment on the horrid contrast of the two forces—anti-human violence and human love.

> He surrenders himself to the pain, not knowing what she (Mumtaz) was trying to tell him, but taking a childish pathetic consolation in the fact that she wanted to be with him wherever he was now going; go with him as she had always wanted to go wherever he went. (p. 369)

Meenakshi Mukherjee believes that both Gian and Debidayal's destinies are shaped by two factors, "the forces of history, and the elements of their personalities. Gian who adapts his policy to suit every circumstance by cringing, deceiving, humiliating himself, bending with every wind, finally withstands the storm, while Debidayal is broken because he refuses to make a compromise with circumstances."[20] But it is the force of history which puts an end to Debidayal in spite of his loftiness, and leaves Gian free in spite of his opportunism.

Malgonkar shows the self-consuming nature of violence through Shafi Usman. The death of his innocent father in the Jallianwala bagh incident turns Shafi to the violent path and soon he becomes the most "wanted" revolutionary. Born a Muslim, he dresses himself as a Sikh which "adds a new significance to the movement." He leads the

Hanuman Physical club which in truth is a freedom fighters's cell. The members of the club, both Muslims and Hindus, renounce all taboos of religion. They eat a curry made of equal parts of beef and pork, thus flouting the sacred impositions of all the religions of India to symbolize unity irrespective of their caste. Shafi stands as a symbol of this secularism.

When Hafiz Khan the top Muslim leader instigates him to turn his back on the Hindus, he shakes his head in dissent to say "It goes against the grain." But Hafiz Khan wields an unconscious influence on his mind and Shafi finally succumbs. When he learns about the police raid, he warns a few members of the club all of whom happen to be Muslims:

> And then he suddenly realised that all those who would be in the club at the time of the raid would be Hindus, there would not be a single Muslim among them. It was the sort of coincidence that worried Shafi for a long time, but even to himself, he refused to admit that it had any thing to do with the visit of Hafiz, or with the clippings he had left behind him. (p. 95)

The sudden change in Shafi was symbolic of what happened to a large segment of the Muslim community at that time. Shafi indulges in senseless violence towards the end and dies as Sundrai hits him magnificently with the statue of Shiva, the God of destruction. Shafi lives and dies in total futility without a sense of fulfilment as a victim of self-defeating violence.

Sundari achieves fulfilment in revenge. She cannot stand hypocrisy and falsity. Her admiration for her brother Debidayal distances her away form Gopal who despises Debi's indulgence in terrorist activities as shameful acts. Both Sundari and Gopal are held "too far apart by their different bonds." As the author comments:

> They were separated even before they were joined together in matrimony, for their marriage was still more than two months away, when the auspicious season would begin. (p. 121)

Gopal's flippant attitude to marriage and his flirting with his girl-friend Malini worsen their relations. Sundari knows his flirtation and feels that their marriage is as good as broken. But she cares little for the imminent break of their marriage.

> Oddly enough, it seemed unimportant. It was almost as though she wanted it so, that she wanted whatever had happened to have happened exactly as it did, so that when the break came, it could be clean and without pain. (p. 151)

Gian becomes significant to her only in terms of his befriending Debi in the jail. Gradually she gets closer to Gian. Seeking fulfilment in revenge on her husband she lies down with Gian at the beach, and offers her husband the same shocking scene which he had created for her with his girl-friend Malini six years ago. It was a measure in retaliation to deliver the death-blow to their marriage. Her fierceness is evident in her act of killing Shafi with the idol of Shiva. She is uncompromising in her quest for fulfilment in revenge.

III

Amur rates *A Bend in the Ganges* superior to *The Princes* as the former has a degree of universality and the latter suffers from being tied down to a set of conservative values.[21] A careful study of Malgonkar's novels including *The Princes*, however, reveals at the core an individual's search for moral identity. History and story may seem to move apart in *A Bend in the Ganges*, as Dayananda believes, especially when the political upheavals and communal riots match ill with the small domestic area within which the characters move.[22] Nevertheless, the sense of incongruity reveals the grim human tragedy with force and violence.

Malgonkar's preoccupation with history is once again evident in his study of Nana Saheb in *The Devil's Wind*. Nana's agonising search for fulfilment imparts a great measure of human interest to the historical narrative.

NOTES

* Manohar Malgonkar, *A Bend in the Ganges* (New Delhi: Orient Paperbacks, 1964). All subsequent references with page-numbers

in parentheses are to this edition.

1. \uthor's Note to *A Band in the Ganges*, 6.
2. James Y. Dayananda, *Manohar Malgonkar* (Boston: Twayne Publishers, 1974) 126.
3. G.S. Amur, *Manohar Malgonkar* (New Delhi: Arnold Heinemann India, 1973) 109.
4. Dayananda 123.
5. Amur 109 and Shyam M. Asnani, "A study of the novels of Manohar Malgonkar," *The Literary Half-Yearly* 16.2 July 1975:91.
6. Ihab Hassan, "The Way Down and Out: Spiritual Deflection in Recent American Fiction," *Virginia Quarterly Review* 39.1 (Winter 1963: 81).
7. Amur 104-05.
8. *New York Times Book Review* 14 Feb. 1965.
9. Dayananda 135.
10. Dayananda 35.
11. Amur 108.
12. Amur 112.
13. Dayananda 131.
14. Shakti Batra, "Two Partition Novels," *Indian Literature* July - September 1975:88.
15. Ram Sevak Singh, "Manohar Malgonkar the novelist," *Indian Literature* 13.1 March 1973.
16. Elena J. Kalinnikova, *Indian English Literature: A Perspective* (Ghaziabad: Vimal Prakashan, 1982) 190.
17. Amur 108.
18. Dayananda 126.
19. S.C. Sood, "The Hero in *A Bend in the Ganges*," *Commonwealth Fiction I*, ed. R.K. Dhawan (New Delhi: Classical Publishing Company, 1988) 198-210.
20. Meenakshi Mukherjee, *The Twice-Born Fiction* (New Delhi: Arnold Heinemann Ltd., 1974) 59.
21. Amur 121.
22. Dayananda 105.

The Devil's Wind

The Devil's Wind deals with the story of Nana Saheb, the controversial figure of the historic Sepoy Revolt of 1857. The event of the Revolt has been a source of many historical and fictional writings both in India and abroad. There are about fifty novels written by English writers on this event.[1] Most of the novels and historical works have depicted Nana as the arch villain of the day, thus reflecting only the British point of view. A representative view of the British could be seen in Pattle's comment:

> Few names are more conspicuous in the annals of crime than that of Nana Saheb, who achieved an immortality of infamy by his perfidy and cruelty at Cawnpore.[2]

However a few historians like Edward Thompson, R.C. Majumdar, Surendrannath Sen have come to the conclusion that there is no dependable evidence to fix the responsibility of the genocide in the Sepoy Revolt upon Nana Saheb. Malgonkar in his endeavour to set the history in correct perspective undertakes to absolve Nana of the false charges. In an interview he says:

> All history of India is written from the British view. Nana Saheb the leading figure of the Mutiny has historically been treated as a villain. In my book . . . I treat him as a human being. I write of him as neither a patriot nor a villain but as a rather mixed-up human being, like most of us are.[3]

Malgonkar's concern is: what makes Nana human, a compound of good and bad. He shows a keen sense of "a feeling for life as it is, in an artistic acceptance of reality."[4] He does not shrink to turn the history of Sepoy

Revolt inside out to reflect on Nana's role in it. He evokes the picture of 1857 with a concern for reality and transforms it into art. Malgonkar has broadened our understanding of the Sepoy Revolt, taking advantage of the novelist's perspective, and also by delving into inner recesses of the mind that most historians fight shy of entering. The novel is a meditation on history and it succeeds as a historical novel by being "a stimulus to the imaginative and critical faculties and an education in human sympathies."[5]

Georg Lukacs writing on history and fiction observes that true realism reveals man and society as complete entities. This precludes exclusive introspection or exclusive extra-version. Realism is therefore "a three dimensionality, an all-roundedness," evoking human relationships in their fullness.[6] Malgonkar does not exclusively give an isolated picture of Nana Saheb. He puts him in proper perspective against the historical background of the Sepoy Revolt. His characters both British and Indian emerge with independent life. He depicts Nana's relationship with the British officers and his commitment to the cause of the country's freedom and tries to place his actions justly under the given circumstances. Although Malgonkar is not original in his historical facts, he adds his imaginative insight to the established historical material for the "clarification of his (Nana's) motives" and his point of view.[7] He succeeds "in restoring to the image of Nana Saheb its basic humanity."[8]

Malgonkar strives to achieve the artistic integration of history and fiction in this novel as he had earlier done in *The Princes*. While *The Princes* deals with the story of the princes in general, *The Devil's Wind* narrows down to focus on the story of Nana Saheb, an individual character of history. In the three parts of *The Devil's Wind*, Malgonkar narrates the personal life of Nana Saheb, his role in the Sepoy Revolt and his last days. As the author assures, the novel "takes no liberaties with verifiable facts or even with probabilities."[9]

Commenting on the limitations of the novel, Amur remarks:

> The Indo-British encounter of which Nana's story is a part, is no longer a matter of vital concern for Indians and Nana has hardly the kind of meaningful symbolism in the context of contemporary life as Camus's Caligula for example has. This perhaps is the central weakness of Malgonkar's book.[10]

It is true that the symbolic aspect of the novel is weak. The novel nevertheless acquires great significance as the psychological story of an individual. The interest of the novel lies in the fervent portrayal of Nana's intense quest for fulfilment which he finds in the values of friendship, patriotism and love. Malgonkar tries to show that Nana has no intentions of cheating either his country or his British friends. He does not want the innocent to be killed gratuitously. He sends word to the Wheelers before his attack on the Entrenchment. During his attacks, violence erupts without his knowledge or involvement. Nana continues his incessant struggle for the freedom of his motherland even after his repeated defeats. Ultimately after his retreat to Nepal, he seeks fulfilment in the love of Eliza, a British girl whom he saved from violence earlier.

II

History in its course tosses up villains and heroes. But not all of them are presented as they in truth were. Facts get perverted and distorted in the hands of the strong and rich to suit their own convenience. Thus heroes become villains and villains heroes. Nana is a victim of this deliberate distortion. His "instinctive squeamishness at the shedding of blood" and "brahminical humanitarianism" were of no consequence to the British. The British have connected him with the crude barbarities of the Bibighar and Satichaura incidents and deliberately made him up into "a monster of ferocity." Nana explains:

> Our revolt had thrown up a surfeit of British heroes but no villains to balance them against, and they needed villainy of the requisite magnitude to serve as a backdrop for heroism. How hollow would Havelock's victories have seemed if I, Nana Saheb, had not been their principal objective! (p. 244)

So the British have magnified the horrors that were already there and invented some and bought a few servants to testify the cooked-up story. They have made Nana into a monster to frighten children with.

Malgonkar defends Nana against the mudslinging of the British by uncovering the hidden facts.

Nana regarded the obligations of friendship as important as those of patriotism and racial loyalty. He had a large number of friends among the British, and he did not wish them to be made into scape-goats for all the wrongs committed by the East India Company. He hesitates to fan the fire of agitation in Kanpur at first. His loyalties were "hopelessly intermixed" between patriotism and friendship, and he could not hate the British whole-heartedly like the others. He did not want innocent men, women and children to become helpless victims of war. He questions:

> Could I now stand by and watch the men and women who had sung and danced and laughed in my house slaughtered by howling mobs? They had done no harm to me, or indeed to India. Why should they have to be sacrificed for all the wrongs piled up by the East India Company over a hundred years? (p. 123)

He is human to the core. He also knew that it would not have been "a surrender to impotence if someone had tried to save the women and children from being butchered." After a good deal of brooding over the question of the rights and wrongs, Nana decides to escort the British families to Bithoor on the request of his collector-friend Hillersdon. Later, however, he is not entrusted with the work. He tries to keep Kanpur unaffected by the Revolt out of compassion for the innocent. He knows that once the Revolt spreads to Kanpur, he has to take part in it whatever the consequences. He believes that he would be "the mediator and the negotiator" and "go down in history as the man who had tempered a Revolt, who had helped his own people to achieve freedom from foreign conquerors with only the minimum bloodletting." (p. 132) One cannot doubt his patriotism for all his affinity with the British officials in India. It is quite ironical that Nana who found the meaning of his life in human values should be linked up with the ghastly happenings in the Revolt and perpetually damned as an assassin in history.

Brought up as the adopted heir of Bajirao II, Nana inherits neither the rich kingdom nor the deplorable frailties of his father. But he seems to have been initiated into brahminical fervour of non-violence by his father's casual remarks in the fencing ground.

> This is only for self-defence, not for killing. Being brahmins, you may not take life. You can kill only in battle—an enemy. But, of course, there are no enemies any longer. Now carry on; smile and don't curse! (pp. 22-23)

After his father's death Nana was just an ordinary citizen indulging in the "undignified wrangle for pension and privileges." All the titles of His Highness Maharaja were snatched away by the British. He did not have even a piece of land to give away as *mahadana* to the priests as part of obsequies of his father. But he suddenly becomes the chosen Peshwa to lead the Revolt in strange circumstances.

Though the Sepoy Revolt had come unawares to the Englishmen in India living "a life of ease, comfort and luxury,"[11] it was a sudden outburst of the long pending impatience gradually nursed among the soldiers and kings against the repressible acts of the British. Malgonkar tries to prove that the Revolt was "a spontaneous explosion of accumulated discontent of the Indian people."[12] The Doctrine of Lapse was just a crude instrument of confiscation evolved by the British to annex the domains of the rulers who died without an heir. The Rani of Jhansi was not allowed to rule for the adopted heir, and her principality was annexed, as was Oudh for maladministration.[13] Efforts were even made to throw away the great Mogul from their ancestral home, the Red Fort. The Mad Mullah and also Zeenat Mahal who was affected by the British refusal to recognise her son as the heir to the Mogul empire, curtained the strategy of revolution. Messages were sent mysteriously in chapaties. Adding fuel to fire came the news that the cartridges greased with the fat of pigs and cows were given to the soldiers. The fear of being converted into "Issahies" also provoked the wrath of the soldiers. In Meerut, Delhi and later at Lucknow, soldiers declined to handle the new cartridges and broke into violence. The incident of Cox firing at the 2nd Cavalry resulting in the death of Nizam Ali, a soldier had led to a revolt under the leadership of Tika Singh. Under these circumstances Nana Saheb was reinstated as the Peshwa of Kanpur by Tika Singh and his followers.

Nana's act of sending word to Wheeler before his attack was prompted by his sense of friendship. He explains:

> I sent him word because I had promised to do so, and I shall never admit that my love for his daughter had anything to do with it. Somehow it seemed important that the gesture be made. . . . *It was my last concession to a friendship I truly valued.* (p. 155) (italics mine)

Nana could not overthrow his obligations as a friend. But his genuine intention to save the innocent men and women turns into an incredibly foolish act as more sepoys and innocent people fell to "mob fury and other grotesque drives of war hysteria." Nana feels sickened by the inhuman impulses of his followers in deciding to starve the people of Entrenchment.

The people of the Entrenchment had to meet a very pathetic plight. With the food supplies stopped from outside, many died, and the second well in the Entrenchment had to be converted into a common grave. Water was rationed at a cupful a day. They had to stoop to the stage of eating even dogs and other animals. When the only thatched barrack was set on fire by Nana Nawab, nearly forty bed-ridden patients were left to die. As many as two hundred and fifty people were killed.

Moved by the predicament of the people in the Entrenchment, Nana assures them a safe passage to Allahabad. He arranges for the manufacture of boats. After a thorough checking, the Englishmen agree for exodus. Many people gathered at the Satichaura Ghat to witness the rulers departing. Balarao, Tantya, Azim and Nana Nawab were to supervise the embarkation.

> Everything had gone off smoothly right till the last moment, in a spirit of tolerance and even good humour—and then there was pandemonium: screams and war cries and the crack and whine of bullets. Even from their vantage point Tantya and others had not been able to see exactly how it started, and once it had started, they too had to make a dash for it and hide in the temple because of the withering fire coming from the boats. (p. 191)

The situation was beyond control and there was a large-scale massacre on the river. No one knew who started it. Having learnt the news, Nana sent messengers to stop the killing and rushed to the spot. By the time he reached the spot, it was too late. Only 170 half-dead men and women were left who were removed to Bibighar. Nana feels intense agony at the unforeseen horror.

> I am sorry, I said to them, but without uttering a sound. This is not how I wanted it to end. Forgive me, I am sorry, sorry, sorry. I have not saved your lives. I have compromised, borrowed a little time for some, perhaps saved a few. I don't know. I am sorry. (p. 194)

Nana's intense anguish could not be expressed.

The Bibighar genocide is another incident with which Nana is wrongly connected. When Nana was camping in Maharajapur preparing for a battle, all the hundred and seventy white women and children held captives at Bibighar were killed. The killing was suspected to have been done by butchers under the directive of Hussainy Begam. Hussainy Begam's daughter was burnt alive in arson at Daryaganj. And the genocide at Bibighar was a measure is retaliation. Even though Nana was not connected with any of these massacres, he was conscientious enough to feel concerned about the Satichaura and Bibighar incidents. He regrets:

> Satichaura and Bibighar are monuments to our brutality. "Look and be ashamed," the world will forever admonish us. "This is what you have done; this is what you are capable of." So long as the sun and the moon go round, our noses will be rubbed in their dregs. (p. 212)

But Nana points to the truth that these incidents are only provocations to the "calculated savagery" of the newly arrived British column headed by Neill and Renaud.

> If Daryaganj and the other villages had not been burned down as guilty villages, Satichaura might never have happened; and if Fatehpur had not been destroyed merely as a follow-through to a victorious military action, Bibighar might never have happened. (p. 212)

The British Column had committed notorious barbarities among the Indian villages just to instil fear by violence. Their motto was— "slaughter all men; take no prisoners." They reduced to ashes the whole villages where they suspected the presence of revolutionaries. Their cruelty was so shocking that people spoke of villages and townships raped, not of a single woman. Referring to the destruction of Lucknow, Nana comments:

> What the British did to Lucknow cannot be balanced against a hundred Satichauras, cannot be washed away by banning all mention of it from history books, cannot be atoned for by a hundred years of the most unblemished administration. It was as though every single soldier was wreaking a personal vendetta against the men, women, and children of the city, and even against its bricks and mortar; the orgy of killing, rape, and vandalism did not abate for weeks. (p. 237)

The British have taken diabolic pleasure in destroying villages only to create a sense of horror. Their crimes cannot be atoned for. The historians have however ignored these while magnifying whatever Indians did.

In the last part of the book, Malgonkar very imaginatively makes Nana Saheb speak out. Here Nana unveils himself. Nana returns to his land to perform his father's *shraddha* ceremony on the bank of the Ganges. There he is recognised by Kashiram Pande, a priest who takes him to Kanpur. To his astonishment Nana finds the inscriptions by the side of the well and the Entrenchment affixing the responsibility of massacres on him, "the rebel Nana" and to "his followers." Nana feels sorry and says that if those who killed were his followers, they would have obeyed his orders to abstain from killing and even harming women and children. He argues that if he is held responsible for the massacres, Queen Victoria should be accused of all the atrocities committed by the British in her name.

> It was a mean, spiteful thing to have put my name on this plaque, implying that I was somehow at the back of it all. On the same principle, should not Queen Victoria's name be inscribed on a thousand monuments in India to suggest that she instigated the atrocities perpetrated by her subjects? (pp. 289-90)

No inquiry could prove that Nana was present anywhere near Bibighar when the tragedy occurred. Whereas hundreds of men had seen Hodson shooting the heirs of the Mogul Emperor, and Fredric Cooper putting forty five people suffocated to death in a congested chamber in Ajnala. Yet they pass off for heroes. Cooper whose toll of victims is nearer five hundred is spoken of as the Hero of Ajnala with impunity, while Nana is chosen as the monster of Bibighar. Nana however does not justify the genocide by the Indian soldiers. He regrets the unfortunate deaths of the British women and children, but concludes that they were "the casualties of war, inevitable in a conflict." (p. 292)

Nana's persistent efforts to fight with the British reveal his patriotic fervour. After liberating Kanpur on 27th June 1857, he loses battles with the British at Fatehpur and Kanpur. His efforts to save the only bridge over the Pandu river fails. In spite of his best strategy, he invariably loses the fights because of the more powerful and wide-ranged weapons of the British. Added to this is the betrayal of his countrymen which Nana could not brook:

> Disgust filled my mind: slaves were assisting their masters to conquer their own mother-land and thus perpetuate their slavery. No country could live down such degradation of its people—we deserved our fate. (p. 235)

In a desperate mood, Nana takes false *jal-samadhi* and disappears in Akbarpur and from there to Chaurasi. But he has not lost all his hopes of regaining his freedom and power. While Tantya Tope, Mani (the Rani of Jhansi), Begam Hazrat Mahal (the Queen of Oudh) continue their attacks on the British, his hopes survive.

> There was still a good chance of the tide's turning—it might turn today, if the Scindia so willed. Then I would join forces with Rani or with the Begam, and one day I would return to Bithoor riding on a white charger. Gangamayi would welcome back the child she had so callously abandoned. (pp. 221-22)

Once in a fit of depression, Nana entertains the thought of ending his life wearing royal dress. But the passing-by soldiers of 43rd Infantry recognise him and extend their support. Suddenly he rises from an ordinary fugitive to the stature of "the commander of an army of five thousand strong." Thereafter he organises numerous attacks against the British. Every time he attains only "nearness to victory," never full victory. Once they could capture the city of Kanpur for a week, forcing General Wyndham to withdraw into his new Entrenchment. But they get defeated in the hands of Sir Colin Campbel, the commander-in-chief. When even his hit-and-run tactics failed, Nana retreats to Nepal where he buys thirteen months of free life with his precious Naulakha necklace.

Nana's unflinching commitment to the cause of his country is stressed in an open letter he wrote to Queen Victoria and her Government in India. He writes:

> "All I want you to understand is that I am not a murderer," I wrote, "but at the same time you have no enemy more determined than myself. *So long as I live, I shall fight.* (p. 270) (italics mine)

Nana has indomitable will to fight for the freedom of his country. But the British Lt. Governor of Oudh in his reply declares Nana an outlaw for his "persistence of rebellion" even though his innocence was proved. Nana is furious at the fact that an Indian could be called an outlaw in his own country. In another letter, he questions:

> "What right have you to occupy India?" I demanded. "How can we accept the argument that you *firanghis* are masters and we 'outlaws' in our own country?" (p. 271)

But Nana, hibernating in Nepal, feels helpless with the news of Tantya Tope's execution by the British and the death of Balarao by the dreadful Terai fever. Jung Bahadur of Nepal writes to the British Resident Colonel Ramsay that Nana had died of Terai fever, and rakes up a controversy about Nana's death. The Britishers display the pictures of Nana on the walls for catching him. Several fake Nanas appeared on the scene to be dismissed later. Nana took no interest in these happenings. With his ambitions wrecked, he could ultimately find his fulfilment in the loving company of his beloved Eliza whom he had earlier saved from the torture of Nizam Ali and his wife. He feels redeemed himself in a state of *nirvana* in her blissful company. He counts his experience with her richer and more satisfying than his past experience and "the master of the wada at Bithoor or as the Emperor's short-lived Peshwa." (p. 296) All his losses are compensated by this domestic bliss.[14] It was almost the bliss of savage life.

> Eliza and I were like some symbolic couples, like Rama and Sita during their exile, finding total fulfilment in one another and hankering for nothing which we could not find in our own surroundings. (p. 275)

He, nevertheless, feels restless at the thought of his native country. He is moved by the sight of his motherland when he returns from Nepal.

> This was my land. My mind would forever be chained to it, my spirit haunts it overlastingly. Wherever I might go, I would never get away from Kanpur. (p. 292)

Nana thus emerges as a man who has relentlessly fought for fulfilment in the values of freedom, friendship and love.

Malgonkar also gives a sensitive portrayal of Nana's private life, the mysterious curse about his marriage, his illegitimate contact with Champa. Nana was initiated into sex by his first concubine Champa. His first wife dies soon after consummation. His second wife dies of cholera. Nana's pretended impotence does not prevent his father from marrying him to another girl, Kashi. Nana, however, abstains from all physical relations with her to save her from the so-called curse.

Nana's relationship with Kashi is quite interestingly portrayed in the novel. It was almost a master-and-slave relationship:

> A wife is a wife, a husband a husband, and they are tied together in one bundle that only death could untie. It was almost a master-and-slave relationship. God knows I did little enough to live up to my obligations as the master; all the same, Kashi made a perfect slave, industrious, diligent, and, above all, loyal. Her unswerving loyalty makes me squirm with guilt—unless that was her way of punishing me, some intuitive, feminine form of revenge. (p. 47)

Kashi was never a woman to Nana. She was just "a piece of furniture" to be displayed on public occasions. She seeks her fulfilment in the womanly instinct of receiving man's love. When she fails to receive it from Nana, she does not hesitate to become a mistress to Jung Bahadur. In a shocking confrontation with Nana, she rebuffs:

> I want to be a woman, not merely a represented freak. I want to live, to become a mother, to experience physical love, violent, abandoned. I want to be in the glitter of a great king's court, not in a hermitage. I'm past twenty and what else was there for me but the prospect of a life-long abstinence, to die before I ever learned to live? (pp. 262-63)

Kashi is almost like the Maharani of *The Princes* in her assertions of the right to live a full-blooded woman's life. Kashi takes revenge on Nana by rejecting him as her husband in turn for having been rejected by Nana as his wife.

Though a minor character in the novel Kashi emerges with power because of her intense quest for fulfilment. It is the same intensity which makes all the mono portraits of the novel vibrate with life. Tantya, a distinguished hero of the Revolt, sheds his last drop of blood for his country's freedom and dies executed by the British. His loyalty for his king is great. Overpowered by grief at Bajirao's death, Tantya drowns himself in a river. When he was rescued, he says: "The master is gone—it is futile to go on living." (p. 48) Tantya's fulfilment is realised in his absolute devotion to his king.

Mani, the Rani of Jhansi, is another fiery force in the freedom fighting. Nana's intention of marrying her was negated by Bajirao's refusal. Nana feels "a sense of loss" all through his life. He thinks it can never be compensated:

> I have never doubted that if Mani had become my wife, my life would have been altogether different—richer, rewarding, exciting. She might not have made me a quiet, properly subservient Hindu wife; but she and I would have made a matched, formidable team, cancelling out the pluses and minuses in our personalities and rounding them off. (p. 28)

But it was only a dream unrealised. Mani was destined to marry "an old and feeble" man. Later she adopts a son and takes the role of "diligent foster mother and the protector and regent of her husband's principality." She finds her fulfilment in being "the grandest rebel" of all the fighters in the devil's wind of the Revolt.

III

Malgonkar is not a mere spinner of tales. He has proved to be a competent student of facts.[15] He recreates the past with its vibrating life. Asnani believes that the novel is "in no case an objective and dispassionate study of history, nor does it bring to the reader's knowledge any new and significant facts."[16] Though Malgonkar reveals the Indian point of view in defending Nana from the attacks of the British historians, one cannot say that it is not dispassionate. Malgonkar points to the horrors committed by both the sides—Indian and the British. He brings out both the virtues and lapses of Nana Saheb. Best has rightly said that Nana is neither "a hero nor an anti-hero, he is the kind of ambiguous character that Malgonkar delights in."[17] Malgonkar presents the argument of Nana as Nana would have written it himself in a cogent way and thus fortifies what is historically true. The historical facts can be interpreted variously. Malgonkar has done his hardest to find the fusion of art and history. He uses his fictional imagination to impart shape to the bare historical facts and bring out the essential human qualities of Nana.

Asnani refers to what he calls historical distortions in the novel and finds fault with Malgonkar's method.[18] Amur on the contrary describes *The Devil's Wind* as "more history than 'novel'."[19] But one should remember that the novel is not all history. Malgonkar makes use of his inventive imagination only where sufficient historical evidence is not available. The end of Nana has always remained a puzzle to the historians. Malgonkar cannot be indicted for historical inaccuracy since fiction rounds off facts, no matter how firmly the author has anchored himself in the historic base.

The Devil's Wind could be contrasted with John Masters's *Nightrunners of Bengal.*[20] Masters in his novel depicts the various events of the Sepoy Revolt in general from the British point of view. But Malgonkar deals with the life of Nana Saheb in particular against the backdrop of the events of the Sepoy Revolt evidently from the Indian point of view. He is understandably not very much pleased with the way Masters has seen "the rebellion as though it were a mutiny."[21] But in fairness it should however be recorded that in the aspects of story-telling and characterisation both of them compel admiration.

The Devil's Wind reveals a deep human sympathy. Malgonkar has achieved a superb integration of history and art in portraying Nana as a moving character in the novel.

NOTES

* Manohar Malgonkar *The Devil's Wind* (New Delhi: Orient Paperbacks, 1972). All subsequent references with page-numbers in parentheses are to this edition.

1. Shailendra Dhari Singh, *Novels on the Indian Mutiny* (New Delhi: Arnold Heinemann India, 1973) 5.
2. A. Miles and A. Pattley. *The Indian Mutiny* (London, 1885).
3. *The Ellsworth American* 12 Nov. 1970.
4. Leon Trotsky, "The Limitations of Formalism," *The Modern Tradition*, ed. Richard Ellman and Charles Feidelson Jr. (New York: Oxford Univ. Press, 1965) 348.
5. Helen Maud Cam, *Historical Novels* (London: Historical Association, 1961) 3.
6. George Lukacs, "Historical Truth in Fiction," *The Modern Tradition*, 351.
7. G.S. Amur, *Manohar Malgonkar* (New Delhi: Arnold Heinemann India, 1973) 125.
8. Amur 134.
9. "Author's Note," *The Devil's Wind* 6.
10. Amur 135.
11. S.D. Singh 16-17.
12. Shyam M. Asnani, "A study of the novels of Manohar Malognkar," *The Literary Half-Yearly* 16.2 July 1975: 92.
13. Singh 15.

14. Amur 131.
15. James Y. Dayananda *Manohar Malgonkar* (Boston: Twayne Publishers, 1974) 139.
16. Asnani 95.
17. Marshall A Best, "Manohar Malgonkar," *Contemporary Novelists,* ed. James Vinson (London: St. James Press, 1973) 826.
18. Asnani 95.
19. Amur 135.
20. John Masters, *Nightrunners of Bengal* (London: Michael Joseph Ltd., 1969).
21. James Y. Dayananda, "On Authors and Books: Interview with Manohar Malgonkar," *The Literary Half-Yearly* 16.2 July 1975: 103.

Conclusion

The study in the foregoing pages reveals Malgonkar's preoccupation with the theme of fulfilment in his novels. Malgonkar's obvious love of plot, story and action in the novel has not impaired his sense of characterization. Malgonkar pits his characters against the backdrop of dramatic action and lets them grow as authentic individuals. It is unfair to call them mere "abstractions," for they emerge with vitality in their agonising quest for fulfilment.

Despite Malgonkar's antipathy to the psychological novel and his preference to be a "spinner of tales," his fiction probes the interior landscape. Psychological depth of characterization is evident particularly in the portrayal of Ruby Miranda, Prince Abhayaraj, Gian, Debidayal and Nana Saheb. The first person narrative (in *The Princes* and *The Devil's Wind*) brings about artistic integration of fact and fiction.

Malgonkar's fiction reveals his intense passion for human values like equality of justice, freedom, and integrity. The protagonists in his fiction seek and obtain a sense of fulfilment in their commitment to these values. Kiran seeks fulfilment in living up to the code of conduct, while Henry Winton fails in his quest because of moral depravity. Ruby Miranda protests violently against the selfish and inauthentic actions of Henry, and her fulfilment lies inevitably in revenge. The efforts of Abhay Raj and his father to preserve the fast-vanishing old feudal order are viewed ironically. Malgonkar rejects both senseless violence and cowardly non-violence in *A Bend in the Ganges*. The novel is however predicated on the theme of redemption in love. Both Gian and Debidayal seek and find fulfilment in their loving commitment to fellow-beings. Nana Saheb's compassion for the innocent British alone redeems him. *The Garland Keepers,* a caustic comment on Emergency in fiction, brings into focus Malgonkar's deep concern for human freedom in peril.

Malgonkar's women characters like Maharani *(The Princes),* Sundari *(A Bend in the Ganges)* and Miranda *(Combat of Shadows)* emerge with power and fervour in confronting their hopeless, almost existential, predicament.

The quest for fulfilment in the fiction of Malgonkar is guided neither by the sociological idealism of Mulk Raj Anand, nor by the philosophical resolution of Raja Rao. Nor does it favour Narayan's ironical resignation to the problems of life. Malgonkar projects an empirical mode without sacrificing dramatic turn of events which sustain the narrative appeal. One would agree with Kalinnikova when she concludes that

> Manohar Malgonkar's works are remarkable phenomenon in modern Indian English literature. Actuality of problems, realistic approach to them, skill to impart dynamism to action, beautiful style—all these put Malgonkar in the ranks of the most popular and readable authors.

Malgonkar's recent fiction *(Shalimar, Open Season, Bandicoot Run)* has perhaps lapsed into entertainment. This does not however diminish the merit of his impressive achievement as a contemporary novelist.

NOTE

1 Elena J. Kalinnikova, *Indian English Literature: A Perspective* (Ghaziabad: Vimal Prakashan, 1982) 191.

Appendix

The Garland Keepers

Malgonkar's latest novel *The Garland Keepers*[1] is an indictment of infringement of human rights and gross abuse of power in Emergency. Though it is in the vein of action packed-entertainers like *Spy in Amber* or *Bandicoot Run,* it acquires distinction on account of the author's quest for truth, individual liberty and social justice. It castigates the power politics of the Great Leader who uses the extraordinary power of Emergency to perpetuate the rule of dynasty aided by selfish, unscrupulous politicians. A shrewd villain like Swami Rajguru finds that no politician is invulnerable to his evil guiles. With the dystopian vision of Orwell, Malgonkar points out that a coterie of yes-men with extra-constitutional authority can hold the country's future to ransom.

India witnessed the rule of Emergency during 1975-77. It was notorious for its excesses through the Press Censorship MISA, indiscriminate implementation of Family Planning and the extra-constitutional authority of a caucus of sycophants. The country as a whole rose up against it to overthrow the government in the subsequent elections. What happened later is, of course, a different story. Although Malgonkar asserts in Author's note to the novel, that the novel is not based on the Emergency of 1975-77, but a "fictional one, supposedly imposed some years later," it is evident that it draws inspiration from these events and is intended to drive home subtly the lesson of Emergency. The passing resemblance is ascribed to the fact that "all fits of national epilepsy must show some common outward symptoms."[2] Further Malgonkar's technique of camouflage through "composite" characters defies close comparison. More than the political personalities, the novel seems to castigate the import of Emergency which has put democracy in jeopardy.

Malgonkar shows with bitter irony that in the rule of Emergency, the entire powet could be used to serve the political ends of the top leaders. Anybody can be arrested, terminated, or promoted depending on his compliance or otherwise with the higher-ups. Seniority "means nothing—not even for that highest judges in the land." (p. 44) Information can either be suppressed, overblown or grossly distorted by manipulating or bullying the media. The Executive, the Judiciary and the Legislature can be nudged to toe the line of the authority by hook or by crook. Freedom, justice, rule of law turn out to be myths in the hands of powerful coterie. Malgonkar projects certain fictitious characters against this backdrop to reveal their moral degeneration. He, however, suggests the hope of resistance to such atrocities through the characters like Om Prakash, Vimal Lal and A.B. Chopra. While the first falls a victim, the latter two succeed in outwitting Rajguru, the root-cause of all evil machinations. Driven out of the country, ironically enough, Rajguru succeeds in preying on the foreign country with his astonishing tact.

The title of the novel is taken from the etiquette of flowers. The epigraph to the novel makes it clear:

> The principal deity in the temples may be garlanded only by the head priest or his deputy, a monarch only by those in the first circle of nobility. When garlands are removed, they are passed on to the most favoured among the courtiers, whose privilege it is to keep them.. . . the etiquette of flowers.

The cunning craftsman Swami Rajguru is the 'head priest'; his chief disciple Ekanti Ma, the Great Leader's son and the 'most dreaded man' *Kalas Kak,* his favourites Kaul and Pashupat known as the Owl and the Pussycat rhyming with their names, from the "Garland Keepers" in the novel. The "Garland Keepers" are criminals amassing black money for the Great Leader and his party without any scruples. The hypocritical Swami Rajguru is the villain of the piece. Kaul and Pashupat enjoy a unique status as the frontmen of the Great Leader and the "surrogate voice of a supreme authority." They run the affairs of the country by transmitting all the orders of the Great Leader to others on phone without keeping anything on record. Rajguru who uses them to his advantage knows their abilities. He tells Surbinder:

> I know that nobody, but nobody, can afford to say no to that pair.

> I have seen ministers quaking and a Lieutenant Governor standing on his head to do their bidding. Surely, even the toughest general will come running with his tail between his legs when he is told that his promotion would be withheld or that his son would never pass his university examination. (p. 155)

The Garland Keepers exposes the treacherous underhand dealings of this caucus.

II

The story of *The Garland Keepers* is interspersed with pungent and ironic comments on the atrocities committed in Emergency. This accounts for the documentary vein of narration in the novel. It also provides an inkling into the novelist's love of freedom and hatred for corruption and dictatorship. Everything is rotten in the state of Emergency. The Police turn out to be puppets in the hands of power-crazy politicians and are put to all sorts of shameful deeds. Batra lists out the indiscriminate disorder perpetrated by the Police:

> You take your orders from palace flunkeys, not from your superiors—and no written orders at that. Two men whom both of us have seen as clerks now crack the whip and you jump, send your minions to plant bootleg whisky or foreign money in someone's house and carry out raids. You bug telephones and put cameras into people's bedrooms to record their sex life. You send perfectly normal people to the loony bin just because they have dared to talk back to that budding Idi Amin who has become your lord and master. You wake up citizens in the middle of the night and march them off to some Gulag horror where you torture them to extract confessions. You hush up a bank fraud of millions because you are terrified of the gang at the top, and then sign blank warrants by the dozen to send innocent people to jails! (p. 15)

The Police are reduced to be the spies of the official party. Reporting the indiscreet utterances of the people is considered a part of their duty according to "the new ethics of the times." The Research and Analysis Wing or RAW and the Directorate of Intelligence Bureau have acquired sinister connotations for this reason. The Police are in fact transformed into an immense, dehumanized machine of master terror." (p. 52) They would unashamedly bulldoze the huts of thousands of poor people overnight to remove "a blot on the face of the city."

The Press which is regarded as the Fourth Estate of Democracy, is also crippled and mauled in Emergency with the censorship. Swami Rajguru and caucus dictate terms to it. The "emasculated and precensored" press filled its space with the doings and pronouncements of the Great Leader and his family members and the advertisements of the Thirty Point Programme. The Party has pampered some papers like *Times* and *Chronicle* which would readily "applaud" the deeds of the government.

Corruption is at the root of the National Democratic Front. The ruling party thrived on black money and abuse of the Emergency powers. The Party's treasurer Atmaram Satham, is a whole-time "slush-fund operator." Restrictions are imposed on traders and film-producers, and they are lifted once the ransom is paid. Kickbacks are secretly received for purchases abroad. Swami Rajguru plays a pivotal role in converting the black money into white, and accruing estates for the Great Leader and his family. The Party does not hesitate to topple Padmakoshal government by the unethical practice of buying nineteen legislators for a million rupees. Ironically the money is paid by Vinay Surana, a big industrialist. The hired tough youngmen are pressed into service for "shouting the proper slogans, ready to create a road block, or to pelt a shop front with stones or start a riot—the party's answer to China's Red Guards." (p. 35) It is named "Dropout Brigade" and led by Ambika Das, an unlettered electric welder who rose to be a powerful political boss. He conducts a weekly "ritual" of showing the loyalty to the Great Leader with his hirelings. The Thirty Point programme is publicised on huge hoardings as if to sedate the public. One is reminded of a situation in Orwell's *1984* with "a barrage of slogans pounded at the proles to keep them under massive sedation." (pp. 52-55)

The jail conditions are abhorrent. Particularly the Tihar jail represents the worst. Visram felt creeps at the thought of "cockroaches and bedbugs in Tihar jail, the filth of its communal laboratories."

Political vendetta has ruled the roost. While compliant officers are rewarded with quick promotions, the duty-bound employees are transferred and arrested on foisted charges under MISA or killed. Om Prakash Agarwal is promoted to be the Deupty Inspector General of Police jumping seniority for quickly disposing Dorabji's case, but he is killed later in an arranged accident for his reinvestigating of the Case. Dorabji is "clinically" killed for leaking out the secrets of black money operation. Visram Lal and AB Chopra, the top Police officials, are relieved of their duties and persecuted. The Bigwigs propose to disconnect the phone, power and water-supply to subdue Netra Agarwal, Om's sister.

What is worse in this situation is the timid compliance of the majority of the people. When they are asked to bend, they crawl. Visram wonders "Why some of his colleagues were helping the very people whom they should be doing their best to put behind bars." (p. 106) Malgonkar's impatience at the meek submission is hinted at in the epigraph from Alexander Solzhenitsyn which reads:

> The strongest chains binding the prisoners were their universal submission and total surrender to their situation as slaves.

However Chopra, Visram and others take cudgels to fight the monumental corruption.

III

The Garland Keepers presents the age-old conflict between the good and the evil. The evil forces are represented by Swami Rajguru, Pashupat and Kaul working for the Great Leader and his son Kalas Kak. Om Prakash Agarwal, Visram Lal, AB Chopra, Batra, Sartaj, Netra Agarwal are on the other side. Malgonkar's portrayal of the characters in the novel is sketchy. Only Swami Rajguru emerges with life. Vimal and Chopra too are portrayed in some detail. The Great Leader is left to be invisible and anonymous as the Big Leader in 1984. Action gets upper hand over the chracterization in the novel.

The action of the novel springs from the crucial Bank Fraud case. Manekji Hormusji Dorabji is convicted with a five-year term of imprisonment for having swindled a bank to the tune of 7 million rupees. But later he demands a fresh trial complaining that "he had confessed under coercion and promises of reward made to him by persons in authority whom he was prepared to name." (p. 4) Cancelling bail, he remains in the jail for fear of threat to his life outside. The young dynamic Deputy Superintendent of Police Om Prakash Agarwal's reinvestigation reveals many skeletons in the cupboard. Mukti Bahini to whom Dorabji was to deliver the money but failed to do so because of the delay in the bank was only a stooge. The Great Leader and the caucus are behind it. Dorabji wonders: "If the Swamiji is at the back, does it mean that the people who have made him their guru also?" (p. 7) Distraught Om approaches Visram, his erstwhile colleague, for advice. But already Om is made a suspect on account of his speediest disposal of Dorabji case and the consequent promotion jumping seniority. So Visram too does not trust him and allow him to confide. Frustrated Om decides to destroy the case diary, but on his way back he is hit by a lorry "deliberately aimed at him" the same night. The Dorabji case proves to be "the kiss of death" as feared by many. It is obvious that the involved higher-ups are out to muffle, the voice of truth by hook or crook.

With the death of Om, Visram steps into his shoes. Kaul and Pashupat try to convert Om's blatant murder into a traffic case caused due to the driving of Om in a drunken state. Visram knew that Om was a tea-totaller all his life. To free Netra from being suspected, he cooks up the false evidence at his flat to give the impression that Om drank with him on the last day and gave him the diary and that he had burnt it. But Pashupat and Kaul are too clever to be trapped. Through the docile new DIG Surbinder, they discover Visram's strategy after their search of the flats of Visram and Netra. Surbinder passes on the smuggled goods kept by Visram in his flat deliberately to Chopra for necessary punishment. Visram now is racked by the same doubts as Om and yearns for advice from a trusted friend. He goes to Chopra who asks him to quit the profession quietly. Visram appears to be a double to Om and it would appear as though Om's fate awaits him. But Visram's clever taping of Om's talk and also Kaul's and Pashupat's telephonic message clears the misunderstanding. Visram and Chopra join hands against the injustice and what follows is a series of moves and countermoves between them, and Rajguru and his followers.

Visram and Chopra are men of integrity. They worked together against the Sopan margi terrorists and won Presidential medals. A leftover from the Raj and an upright and hardworking officer, Chopra remained a hard nut to crack for the politicians in power. Close to retirement he is made the Chief of Investigations (COI) in the Special Branch of Police and had little to do with the day to day problems of law and order. Visram, Superintendent of Police, is an honest officer trained in Interservices Commando school. Both Vimal and Chopra have an uncompromising commitment to truth and work in unison to expose the highest echelons of power.

An individual pitted against the whole machinery of the Government, Visram faces several obstacles in his investigation. He could infer from Dorabji the involvement of Ekanti Ma, Kaul and Pashupat in commuting the black money. But before he could make any headway, Dorabji is killed, poisoned "by new fangled toxins into blood." Visram also fails to get the diary from Netra Agarwal because she would not trust him. Her brother rang her up before his death and asked her not to give the diary to Visram because he was not trustworthy. It is only after he rescued her at El Taj from the clutches of Ambika Das that she comes to trust him. She tells him that she hid diary in the safe of the Parliament street office of the Surana Company where she worked. But it is too late as all the Surana offices are just then raided without any notice and the files along with the diary confiscated. Chopra's discovery of two lists in the raid however throws new light on the ruling party's collection of unaccounted donations to the tune of 5 million rupees from big Industrialists and their unethical game of buying of nineteen MLAs of Padmakoshal state to topple the government. Chopra suspects Rajguru's role in this.

Rajguru in the other camp knows each and every movement of Visram and Chopra through the network of Surbinder. He decides to put them out of the way. Warrant is issued to arrest Visram who escapes to Kasauli and from there to the secret military refuge with the help of Avinash Batra of Dirty Dogs. Chopra is eased out of his office on a false charge of CIA connection. The three hard-boiled professionals—Vimal, Chopra, Batra—are brought together "by nothing so much as a shared service ethic and trust in each other's integrity and professional skill." (p. 122) Under the leadership of Chopra, they decide to fight the evil forces unitedly. They are now certain who the culprits are in the black money operation.

> From the outset, it was clear who the principals were: Rajguru and that woman he calls his chief disciple, Ekanti Ma. And they were aided and abetted by Kaul and Pashupat. (p. 124)

Chopra gathers another secret from the newspaper cutting sent him by his sister from America, that Gatwick Aircraft Company did not gift the aircraft to Rajguru as publicised but sold even without discount. He suggests:

> What I think we should do is to go and beard the man—tell him all that we have found out. Get the swine rattled. Then wait for him to make his move. At least we shall have deprived him of his principal weapon: inaction. Don't you see—we must make him act, come out into the open. (p. 133)

Chopra chalks out the strategy to encounter Rajguru.

IV

Swami Rajguru is an octogenarian yoga teacher who rose to be the spiritual master of the Great Leader and the closest friend of his son. He has kept himself "firm, supple and healthy" with his yoga in spite of his age. His leanings are towards the rich and the influential to whom he teaches yoga and tantra. An opium-addict, he is marked by lust and avarice. Young girls in see-through linen are employed at the ashram to serve him. Beautiful young ladies alone have the privilege of treatment there. Ironically his motto is: "Through yoga to full enjoyment of his life." (p. 61) The ashram acquired the image of being a school for the teaching of Kamasutras. The mysterious death of his earlier secretary in a fire accident smacked of a sex scandal. He is obsessed with mad desire for his specially chosen new secretary Vanita Dave, and tempts her at last with the offer of a free trip to Europe with him. He is a Machiavellian craftsman to whom nothing is impossible. His highly inaccessible and guarded ashram is built in a sprawling six-acre wooded plot with si bungalows designed by the German architect Rainer Storch. Highly-privileged land set aside for an artificial limb centre was grabbed for car parking by dismissing the complainant and imprisoning him on a charge of being anti-government. It was established that

> Swami Rajguru was a highly-privileged person, that any favour done to him by officials would not go unrewarded, and that anyone whom the Swami found uncooperative be shown no mercy. (p. 57)

Even the Air Force was made to withdraw the complaint of "grave security risk" in locating the ashram in their vicinity. The problem was solved by building a high wall between the ashram and their range. But Swami went on an offensive and got the proposal to shift the Air Force establishment elsewhere accepted.

Swami's importance in the affairs of the administration and the party is due to two reasons: (a) his closeness to the Great Leader, (b) his possession of microfilm library of the secret dossiers of men and women prominent in the nation's life. It was in fact the brain-child of Shamkant Sen, a Junior Minister who used to tell:

> Power does not come out of the barrel of a gun. . . . In democracies it flows from your knowledge of your rival's secrets. (p. 95)

But Sen was killed in an accident suspected of foul play. Swamiji tactfully procures the microfilmed secret files from the new minister Udamrao Maney by convincing him with his discourse on Chanakyan philosophy and inadequacy of Gandhian ideology. One should have the power to compel people to do things against their inclinations.

> Oh, only once is a long while—but naturally. Still, the power must be there, in the hands of someone who is above self-interest, someone who can be trusted never to abuse it . . . never! (p. 96)

As a reward Udamrao who always lost elections was granted his wish of becoming a diplomat with a "a foreseeable future of duty-free wines and cigars and tax-free salary." (p. 96)

The anti-climax for Rajguru begins with the countermoves of

Chopra, Visram and Batra who outwit him in craft and cunning. Visram goes to Rajguru's ashram as Girija Shankar, an opposition M.P., who was arrested in the demonstration before Parliament and sent to Tihar Jail. He tells Rajguru that he had met Dorabji at the jail and learnt from him their secret transactions. He offers to be a paid courier to him like Dorabji. Rajguru is nonplussed at the proposal. In the course of conversation Rajguru receives a phone call from Chanakyapuri police station that the messenger at his house is Visram Lal and they would arrest him within ten minutes. Visram's arrest however turns out to be a mock-arrest. Rajguru is hoodwinked. He receives the first setback.

Rajguru now makes all-out efforts to trace Visram. Surbinder gathers that Visram is in the army hush-hush section but fails to discover the location as it is an army secret. Rajguru is angry and Surbinder's hopes of getting permanent promotion are dashed. Rajguru cleverly taps the information from D.C. Bose, former Director of Intelligence, who was known as "Blankets Bose" for his misappropriation of American blankets meant for flood-victims. Visram is attacked at his refuge, but Sartaj incidentally comes to his rescue.

Through Sartaj a new dimension of Rajguru's past is revealed. Sartaj was sent by Om Prakash to Kashmir to collect some evidence which was regarded by him as "my ace of trumps." According to this information, Rajguru joined the Order of the Thirteen at Deoban Math impersonating Lama Pulakashi whom he had killed along with Angaraka, and later spent fifty years at Tashi Lunpo monastery. He became Rajguru only after his entry into Delhi. This information leads to the stunning discovery that Rajguru was actually Naik Fida Ali, a Pakistani soldier who suffered humiliation under the homosexual Captain Jamal Din and deserted the army on 8th April 1948. This event is recorded in the novel in the Prologue. Malgonkar keeps it in suspense till the end.

The denouement comes off in the form of Chopra's elaborate strategy involving the Defence personnel to repatriate Rajguru to the Pakistani army for court-martialling and get rid of the country's worst politician. While Netra engages Kalas Kak, Rajguru and others at El Taj, his car is used by Visram, Batra and Sartaj in saffron guru shirts to enter Rajguru's ashram uninhibited. They blast he inner shrine the sound of which is overwhelmed in the arranged crashes of the Air Force. The Microfilm Dossier, the secret of Rajguru's strength, is picked.

On the fateful day, Visram lands in the ashram from a helicopter like a "superman" and holds Rajguru and Ekanti Ma at gunpoint. The encounter is a mirror to Rajguru's mean tactics in his desperate bid to save his life. Upset by the fact that his dossier is snatched, he tries to coax Visram, lure him with money and bully him.

> What is it to you if I and a few friends have worked out a method of siphoning off some of the funds which are illegally obtained in any case? And how do you know that those who are in charge of the funds are not our accomplices? Have you ever stopped to think that something which became apparent to outsiders like you and Chopra is not known to the Great Leader? Could vast funds have been sent abroad without the Great Leader's knowledge and even connivance? Have you not heard of the chain of motels in Canada that Kakji owns, the five-star hotel on the shore of lake Garda that is coming up?—the family's vast holdings in multinational companies? (pp. 192-193)

Rajguru uses all his tact to direct Visram's anger to the Great Leader and provokes him that he

> has already become resigned to the perpetuation of dynasty, an absolute monarchy complete with an heir apparent. Above all, his official blinkers do not permit him to look upon people like ourselves as benefactors of society, as those who are doing their mite to sabotage the brazen attempts at imposing dynastic rule. Oh, no! He is horrified. To him we are criminals because we have taken money that does not belong to us. (p. 193)

He dreads to face his sinful past. The final revelation of his identity as Naik Fida Ali comes off with cataclysmic force. Rajguru is now ready to beg him not to hand him over to the Pakistani military:

> Don't you know what barbaric punishments they dole out for the commonest offences?—like chopping off your hands and feet? Come on, you bastard! Kill me—kill me if you dare! (p. 196)

But Rajguru is dropped from a plane in the deserts two hundred miles away to the charge of General Jamal Din.

Rajguru's unmatching resourcefulness and foresight are revealed in the Epilogue. He has made best use of the few seconds of privacy given him with Ekanti Ma. Through her he has arranged to convey to the Chief of Pakistani Field Marshall Inayat Usman about his possession of secret files of all the VIPs of India. He had with foresight preserved a set of the Microfilms at Switzerland. The novel ends with the Field Marshall's invitation to him to the Presidential suite for consultations. Rajguru does not hesitate to mortgage the country's destiny for his personal gain.

The novel ends on an ambivalent note. Visram's plan suggests the secret support of the Defence Minister. The possibility of dethronement of the Great Leader is not ruled out. This positive note is however marred by Rajguru's success. What Malgonkar wants to suggest is that Emergency transforms a country into a dystopian nightmare with the corrupt politicians.

Malgonkar makes the plot interesting by employing the political intrigue, moves and countermoves involving interesting codes to evade detection, irony and suspense. The interspersing of the plot with insightful remarks on fictional Emergency renders the novel occasionally documentary. Malgonkar also uses Hindi words like *chalo, bhaijan, sandhya, shaitan, bhenchod, Baapre, bakwas, dagabaz*. Some of these words reveal the vulgarity of new generation politicians. Although *The Garland Keepers* is not Malgonkar's best, it is an interesting novel which reveals his passionate quest for freedom and justice.

NOTES

1. Manohar Malgonkar, *The Garland Keepers* (New Delhi: Vision Books, 1986). All subsequent references with page numbers in parentheses are to this edition.
2. "Author's Note," *The Garland Keepers.*

A Select Bibliography

I PRIMARY SOURCES

(a) Novels:

Distant Drum. Delhi: Hind Pocket Books, 1960.
Combat of Shadows. Delhi: Orient Paperbacks, 1962.
The Princes. Delhi: Hind Pocket Books, 1970.
A Bend in the Ganges. New Delhi: Orient Paperbacks, 1964.
The Devil's Wind. New Delhi: Orient Paperbacks, 1972.
The Garland Keepers. New Delhi: Vision Books, 1986.

(b) Entertainments:

Spy in Amber. Delhi: Hind Pocket Books, 1971.
Open Season. Delhi: Orient Paperbacks, 1978.
Shalimar. Delhi: Orient Paperbacks, 1978.
Bandicoot Run. New Delhi: Orient Paperbacks, 1982.
Garland Keepers. New Delhi: Vision Books.

(c) Short Stories:

Malgonkar, Manohar. *A Toast in Warm Wine*. New Delhi: Hind Pocket Books, 1974.
Bombay Beware. New Delhi: Orient Paperbacks, 1975.
Rumble Tumble. New Delhi: Orient paperbacks, 1977.

(d) Play:

Line of Mars. Delhi: Hind Pocket Books, 1978.

(e) Histories:

Kanhoji Angrey, Maratha Admiral: An account of his life and his battles with the English. Bombay: Asia Publishing House, 1959.

The Sea-Hawk. New Delhi: Vision Books, 1978.

The Puars of Dewas Senior. Bombay: Orient Longman, 1963.

Chatrapatis of Kolhapur. Bombay: Popular Prakashan, 1971.

(f) Non-fiction:

The Men who Killed Gandhi. Madras: Macmillan, 1978.

Cue from the Inner Voices: The Choice before Big Business. New Delhi: Vikas, 1980.

II SECONDARY SOURCES

(a) Books:

Amur, G.S. *Manohar Malgonkar.* New Delhi: Arnold Heinemann India, 1973.

Asnani, Shyam M. *Critical Response to Indian English Fiction.* Delhi: Mittal Publications, 1985.

Cam, Helen Maud. *Historical Novels.* London: Historical Association, 1981.

Daiches, David. *The Novel and the Modern World.* Chicago: The Univ. of Chicago Press, 1970.

Dayananda, James Y. *Manohar Malgonkar.* Boston: Twayne Publishers, 1974.

Forster, E.M. *Hill of Devi.* London: 1953.

Gokak, V.K. *English in India: Its Present and Future.* Bombay: Asia Publishing House, 1964

Iyengar, K.R.S. *Indian Writing in English.* Bombay: Asia Publishing House, 1973.

Kalinnikova, Elena J. *Indian English Literature: A Perspective,* ed. K.K. Sharma, Trans. Virendra Pal Sharma. Ghaziabad: Vimal Prakashan, 1982.

Kumar, S.K. and Mckean, K. ed. *Critical Approaches to Fiction.* New

York: McGraw-Hill Book Company, 1968.

Lukacs, George. *The Historical Novel.* London: Merlin Press, 1962.

Machwe, Prabhakar. *Four Decades of Indian Literature: A Critical Evaluation.* New Delhi: Chetna Publications, 1976.

Masters, John, *Bhowani Junction.* London: Michael Joseph, 1961.

———————. *Nightrunners of Bengal.* London: Michael Joseph Ltd., 1969.

Miles, A. and A. Pattle. *The Indian Mutiny.* London: 1885.

Mohan, Ramesh, ed. *Indian Writing in English.* New Delhi: Orient Longman, 1978.

Morris, John. *Eating the Indian Air.* New York: Atheneum, 1969.

Mukherjee, Meenakshi. *The Twice-Born Fiction.* New Delhi: Arnold Heinemann India, 1971.

Naik, M.K., S.K. Desai and G.S. Amur, ed. *Critical Essays on Indian Writing in English.* New Delhi: Macmillan, 1968.

Naipaul, V.S. *An Area of Darkness.* England: Penguin Books, 1975.

Narsimhaiah, C.D. *The Swan and the Eagle.* Simla: Institute of Advanced Study, 1970.

Parameswaran, Uma. *A Study of Representative Indo-English Novelists.* New Delhi: Vikas Publishing Pvt. Ltd., 1976.

Rao, Raja. *Kanthapura.* Madras: Oxford Univ. Press, 1974.

Singh, Shailendra Dhari. *Novels on the Indian Mutiny.* New Delhi: Arnold Heinemann India, 1973.

The Directory of British and American Writers, 1971.

Verghese, Paul. *Problems of the Indian Creative Writer in English.* Bombay: Somaiya Publications, 1971.

Narsimhan, Raji. *Sensibility under Stress: Aspects of Indo-English Fiction.* New Delhi: Ashajanak Publications, 1976.

(b) Articles

Asnani, Shyam. "A study of the novels of Manohar Malgonkar." *The Literary Half-Yearly* 16.2 July 1975: 71-98.

Batra, Shakti. "Two Partition Novels." *Indian Literature* 18.3 July-Sept. 1975: 83-103.

Best, Marshall A. "Manohar Malgonkar." *Contemporary Novelists,* ed. James Vinson. London: St. James Press, 1973: 824-26.

Chaddah, R.P. "The Partition in Indo-Anglian Fiction." *The Journal of Indian Writing in English* 5.2 July 1977: 52-58.

Chinneshwararao, G.J. "Anand's *Private Life* and Malgonkar's *The Princes.*" *The Journal of Indian Writing in English* 4.1 Jan. 1976: 15-21.

Cotton, John, "John Masters." *Contemporary Novelists,* ed. James Vinson. London: St. James Press, 1973: 850-52.

Cowasjee, Saros. "The Princes in Indian Fiction." *Kakatiya Journal of English Studies* 2.1 Spring 1977: 48-70.

Dayananda, James Y. "Rhythm in Manohar Malgonkar's *The Princes.*" *Literature East and West* 15.1 March 1971: 55-73.

———. "M. Malgonkar's *The Devil's Wind.*" *World Literature Written in English* 2.2 Nov. 1972: 112-15.

———. "The Initiatory Motifs in M. Malgonkar's *The Princes.*" *MAHFIL, A Quarterly of South Asian Literature.* 8.2-3 June-Sept. 1972: 223-35.

———. "An Interview with Manohar Malgonkar." *Lock Haven Review* 14 (1973): 78-102.

———. 'M. Malgonkar' *The Devil's Wind.*" *Literature East and West* 15.3 March 1973: 523-25.

———. "On Authors and Books: An Interview with Manohar Malgonkar." The Literary Half-Yearly 16.2 July 1975: 99-107.

———. "Manohar Malgonkar on his novel *The Princes:* An Interview" *Journal of Commonwealth Literature* 9.3 : 21-28.

———. "The Image of Women in Manohar Malgonkar's Novels." *Journal of South Asian Literature* 12.3 & 14.

Dwivedi, A.N. "The Historian as Novelist: Manohar Malgonkar." *Perspectives on Indian Fiction in English.* New Delhi: Abhinav Publishers, 1985: 135-49.

Hassan, Ihab. "The Way Down and Out: Spiritual Deflection in Recent American Fiction." *Virginia Quarterly Review* 39.1 Winter 1963.

Iyengar, K.R.S. "The Role of the Writer and Critic Today." *Indian Literature* Jan-March 1975: 31-41.

Jain, Jasbir. "Vishnu and Shiva: Symbols of Duality in *A Bend in the Ganges.*" *Journal of Indian Writing in English* 3.1: 21-24.

James, Henry. "The Art of Fiction." *American Literature Survey: Nation and Religion* 1860-1900, ed. Stern, M.R. and S.L. Gross. New Delhi: Light and Life Publishers, 1975: 323-44.

Jayashri, I. "Women versus Tradition in the Novels of Manohar Malgonkar." *Triveni* 45.2 July-Sept. 1976: 73-80.

Lukacs, Georg. "Historical Truth in Fiction." *The Modern Tradition*, ed. R. Ellman and Ch. Feidelson Jr. New York: Oxford Univ. Press, 1965: 349-60.

Malgonkar, Manohar. "Purdah and Castemarks." *The Times Literary Supplement* 4 June 1964: 491.

NandaKumar, Prema. "Indian Writing in English: 1972-73" *Indian Literature* Oct.-Dec. 1974: 77-97.

New York Times Book Review 14 Feb. 1965.

"Ruling Passions." *The Times Literary Supplment* 21 June 1963: 457.

Sharma, D.R. "Manohar Malgonkar and the Satpura Code." *Quest* 100 March-April 1976: 51-58.

Singh, Khushwant. "Outstanding Books: 1947-77." *The Illustrated Weekly of India* 98.33 14-20 Aug. 1977: 45.

Singh, Ram Sevak. "Manohar Malgonkar, the Novelist." *Indian Literature* 13.1 March 1973.

Shankar's Weekly 25 June 1961.

Sood, S.C. "The Hero in *A Bend in the Ganges*." *Commonwealth Fiction*, ed R.K. Dhawan. New Delhi: Classical Publishing Company, 1988: I, 198-210.

The *Ellsworth American* 12 Nov. 1970.

"The Kipling Heritage." The Times Literary Supplement 12 May 1961: 289.

Trotsky, Leon. "The Limitations of Formalism." *The Modern Tradition*, ed. R. Ellman and Ch. Feidelson. New York: Oxford Univ. Press, 1965: 340-49.

Walsh, William. "Nataraja and the Packet of Saffron: The Indian Novel in English." *Readings in Commonwealth Literature*. London: Clarendon Press, 1973: 51-57.